Chapman

KV-374-651

– Poetry at War – A New Scotland Speaks –

Illustrations by Hugh Bryden, John MacWilliam and David Stephenson.

ISBN 0 906772 90 7   ISSN 0308-2695   © *Chapman* 1999

CHAPMAN

4 Broughton Place, Edinburgh EH1 3RX, Scotland
E-mail: editor@chapman-pub.co.uk
Website: www.chapman-pub.co.uk
Tel 0131–557 2207 Fax 0131–556 9565

Editor: Joy Hendry   **Assistant Editor: Gerry Stewart**

Volunteers: Valerie Brotherton, Marie Carter, Hannah Ekberg, Serena Field, Pat Fox, Helen Galliard, Andrea Gourgy, Jenny Hadfield, and Maryann Ullman.

Submissions:

Chapman welcomes submissions of poetry, fiction and articles provided they are accompanied by a stamped addressed envelope or International Reply Coupons

Subscriptions:

	Personal		Institutional	
	1 year	2 years	1 year	2 years
UK	£16	£30	£20	£38
Overseas	£21/$35	£39/$65	£25/$43	£47$75

THE SCOTTISH **ARTS** COUNCIL

Printed by Inglis Allen, Middlefield Road, Falkirk FK2 9AG

Editorial

One of the dominant themes of this century, as far as poetry is concerned, is the emergence of war poetry almost as a separate genre. The poets of World War One used poetry as a way of changing the general sensibility about the nature of war, putting a huge question mark over martial patriotism for subsequent generations. It was no longer taken for-granted that it was intrinsically glorious to die for your country; the ideal of heroism as a virtue in itself became quite rightly tarnished forever. That hasn't stopped wars, nor has it stopped both men and women signing over their lives for causes, whether right or wrong. But at least in people's minds, this possibly fatal act has lost much of its glamour. Poetry hasn't stopped wars, but it has accomplished something now, I hope, irreversible

In this *Chapman*, Angus Calder takes this phenomenon several steps further, by asking questions about the relationship between poetry and war. Things have moved on: the poetry stemming from World War Two has been marginalised by that of the First War, which, ironically, has acquired an unjustified poetic glamour. To mark the difference in sensibility between the two wars, the poet Tom Scott amending Owen's words says that the poetry was not in the pity, but in the understanding. We do understand a little more now, and the poetry of the Second War reflects that. We need look no further than the work of our own Sorley MacLean and William Soutar. The ongoing conflict in the Balkans has produced a remarkable poetic response, which Calder examines here, focusing on *Scar in the Stone*, an anthology of Balkan writing, and *Cold Night Lullaby* by Colin Mackay, published by *Chapman*. His central question concerns the extent to which poetry can be a reliable witness to acts of atrocity and genocide.

The other main theme in this issue is a response to our new devolved Parliament, something which *Chapman* has, in a non-partisan way, argued for consistently over many years. Here, Nigel Grant, writing in Scots, debates the way in which the Scottish Parliament can distinguish itself from some of Westminster's more moribund traditions and locate itself in practices which are simultaneously more amenable to Scottish intellectual and cultural traditions, and also more modern, appropriate to the 21st century. Adding to these thoughts is the article by Graeme Orr, reflecting on what Scotland could learn from the experience of Slovakia. But perhaps most telling is the piece by Tom Nairn which is very difficult to define: it's not a critical article, not a sustained argument, but a curious cross between personal reflection and fiction. But there is nothing fictional about the thrust of it, which issues a challenge to the Scottish people, in particular the media, to grapple with the many cultural, political and social questions which now face us, slamming the sham journalism which continues to get in the way of genuine, vital debate.

Finally, and tragically, this issue celebrates the artistic work of the mercurial and multi-talented John MacWilliam, who died in April this year aged 37. John was a unique and very special person whose contribution to Scotland was remarkable and unpredictable. His art appeared in *Chapman* many times, and his versatility is demonstrated in the illustrations reproduced here as a tribute, and as thanks for his long dedication to the magazine. One of the most outstanding is his portrait of the poet George Campbell Hay, commissioned for *Chapman* 58, culled from photographs. This shows an incredible sensitivity and understanding, capturing so much of the nature of the complex and tormented poet, whom he had never met. I worked with John on the design and layout of *Astronauts and Tinklers*, a book of poems and drawings by Wendy Wood, and its template became the examplar for our subsequent books of poetry.

He was essentially mischievous and anarchic, as is evident in the cartoons he did for the magazine. His subjects were not always pleased by the result, but we always were. Most recently, he provided satirical cartoons for *Chapman*, responding to the provocative nature of Jon Corelis's article in No 87, on the nature of British poetry, and also for No 92, featuring some vehement responses to that article. Corelis thought so much of John's cartoon that he purchased the original, which pleased John greatly.

It is impossible to sum John up in a few words. As an artist, he had enormous talent, but, alas, often neglected this. He lived a difficult life, being essentially freelance, having to grasp whatever opportunities came his way, in teaching, in journalism and other exploits. In one way he was one of the easiest people to work with I've ever met. When commissioned on a project he would work at short notice, always giving his penetrating attention to the nature of it. In producing the Corelis artwork, he took the trouble to telephone Corelis in San Francisco, just to chat about the basic ideas. He could also be very difficult, but in the best way possible. He took no prisoners, wasn't afraid to provoke people, couldn't be fobbed off by woolly thinking and was extremely demanding both of himself and others. He was uncompromising in his relations with other people, being unafraid to give even close friends their character, no holds barred and often with a cuttingly rebarbative remark. Rank, status, reputation cut absolutely no ice with him, and he wasn't afraid to be wicked – in my experience always with good reason – to those who were 'asking for it'. He was also exceptionally loyal and self-critical, always re-evaluating both himself and others. He had a naughty sense of humour. One day, having just acquired a mobile phone and being stupidly technophobic about it, I was sitting in the pub, not having noticed John sitting nearby. Suddenly my phone rang, and I fumbled uselessly with it, then looked up to see John, wagging his phone at me and grinning.

His last project was to set up his own school, teaching mainly English as a foreign language. It is even more tragic that he died just as this was about to get off the ground. Thankfully, it is now up and running, benefiting from the meticulous organisation and preparation which occupied him the last year of his life. His family, and his friends and colleagues are still reeling from his death, lamenting the many original and productive things which otherwise would have come from this exceptional man.

Self-Portrait, John MacWilliam

Poetry and War

Angus Calder

On 11 July, 1995, the town of Srebrenica, supposedly a UN 'safe area', was taken by Bosnian Serbs whose forces had invested it for three years. In the next few days 7,000 Bosnian males were massacred and the remaining non-Serb population driven out. Eventually Bosnia became a fraught, but 'peaceful' UN protectorate. But the Bosnian Serb leaders, Radovan Karadzic and General Ratko Mladic, indicted for genocide by the Tribunal for War Crimes at the Hague, remained at large. The Yugoslav state, dominated by the Serbs, went on to perpetrate further 'ethnic cleansing' against the overwhelmingly Albanian population of the province of Kosovo.

In The Heart of Europe, a Belfast-published booklet, four poems stand beside striking prints by a Mexican, Irish-based artist, is a response to the Balkan crisis. Alfonso Lopez Monreal's images evoking the ordeal of Sarajevo, such as civilian sufferers stripped of their skin, are named 'Desastres', after Goya's 'Disaster of War', a response to the horrors of the Napoleonic era. Nuala Ní Dhomhnaill's poem in Irish Gaelic, 'Dubh' (*'Black'*) is a direct response to the fall of Srebrenica. The event eclipses everything:

> The spuds are black.
> The turnips are black.
> Every last leaf of cabbage in the pot is black.

Northern Ireland's decades of crisis resound in 'Fleur De Lis' (Bosnia's national emblem) by the booklet's co-editor Chris Agee, an American poet domiciled in Belfast. Harry Clifton's 'The Literal Version' explores the problem of rendering into an alien language another's experience of the world. The last poem, 'Reassurance' by Bernard O'Donoghue is accomplished, but its implications worry me. It begins with a wife assuring her dying husband that heaven certainly exists, and goes on:

> Personally, I hope not. Because, if Hell and Heaven
> Are assorted by the just God we learnt of,
> We can have little prospect of salvation:
> We who have just turned on the sports news,
> Leaving the hanged girl from Srebrenica
> On the front page, just as before we watched
> Without a protest while the skeleton soldier
> Burned by the steering wheel on the road to Basra:
> We too who are so sure about the frailties
> Of those who failed to do anything about
> The Famine, or who'd turn up the volume
> To drown the clanking of the cattle trucks
> That pulled away eastward in black and white.

This seems to demonstrate why poets should leave particular statements about certain issues to journalists, photographers, film-makers, pamphleteers, historians and theologians. Ní Dhomhnaill's forceful personal reaction, politically highly charged, shows what poetry can do. It is like Neruda's acclaim for the International Brigade in 'The Battle of the Jarama River'. Such direct, passionate responses beg no questions and pretend no answers.

O'Donoghue refers, inexactly, to a controversial front-page picture of an Iraqi soldier in the Gulf War reduced to a cinder. His suggestion that if Heaven exists we would not deserve to enter it because we have not responded to Srebrenica is sociologically preposterous, theologically frivolous and rhetorically unpersuasive. During a decade of Balkan conflict terrible massacres have resulted from political breakdowns in Africa, Indonesia, Algeria; the Russians have savaged Chechnya without UN intervention; mass murderers have remained at large in Cambodia. Those who believe, as I do, that international action had to be taken against the Serbia of Milosevic, his eggers-on and his accomplices must accept that many other monsters deserve chastisement. If God exists, He or She would see support for action on this front cause for mercy.

I think that O'Donoghue does not believe in God or Heaven. 'Thou shalt respond at once and completely to all suffering' would be a perverse Commandment anyway. Someone who spent all her or his time agonising over distant atrocities would be useless to family, friends, associates and compassionate bystanders. People besieged in Sarajevo yearned for precisely the daily pleasures and little decencies enjoyed by denizens of peaceful places. As in Ní Dhomhnaill's '*Black*', shock and outrage may for a time overshadow such considerations completely. But 'life goes on'.

Perhaps the most ancient subject of poetry is war. Ironically, the South Slav area, in which the recitation from memory of ancient epics has been in modern times a communal custom, has provided models for scholars studying the origins and transmission of the epic poems eventually written down as *The Iliad* and *The Odyssey*. Epic was until recently regarded as the most serious and important sort of poetry, but the epic may have fed Serbian racism. In our century, epic treatment of war has become impossible. 'War Poetry' has emerged, a genre reserved for men at arms and civilians directly caught up in conflict. 'Anti-war Poetry' is another new genre, a species of committed verse. Christopher Logue's versions of parts of *The Iliad*, which 'deconstruct' Greek heroism, are in effect 'anti-war poems'.

'Committed' or 'protest' poetry has proliferated. The stripped simplicity of Brecht has often been a disastrous model. The Women's Movement has engendered much valuable verse. Powerful Black Power voices rose in the USA in the 1960s and black people resident in Britain have produced effective poetry about racism and its effects. But this, often delivered in performance, raises, at its less-than-best, a critical problem I associate above all with verse by black South Africans. One irony of the apartheid era was that white publishers were allowed to print masses of protest poetry by black, 'coloured' and white writers. The authorities conceded thus to assure their open and tacit supporters in the USA and Britain that 'freedom of the press' prevailed, and because they judged that poems (and such plays as Athol Fugard's) would not damage their regime. As Auden said in his 'In Memoriam W B Yeats', poetry "makes nothing happen". Brecht could not bring down Hitler, nor could Neruda save Allende.

South African protest poetry thumped the themes of white oppression and violence, black suffering and the need for resistance. Mongane Wally Serote, who showed that major poetry could be based on these themes, was forced into exile. Lesser writers remained free in South Africa. Their verse, read aloud at public meetings, may have had a direct, useful effect. Much of it, to an outsider, seemed to be mediocre or bad verse. Topicalities and current concerns handled in most 'committed' poetry would be better served by good prose, well-written rapportage, articles and pamphlets. Good 'political' poetry does not have immediate results, but people remember it for decades. Yeats's 'Easter 1916' helped to rally opinion in favour of Irish independence, but its long-term, more important effect was to assist the mythologisation of the Rising's leaders. American corporations producing fruit in Latin America have recently bared their claws in the tariff war against EU preference for Caribbean banana growers. So Neruda's 'United Fruit Co.' is as topical as ever, half a century later – because what it willed to 'happen', the overthrow of exploitation, has not happened. The best articles and pamphlets are usually out of date in weeks, months or years. Wilfred Owen's 'war poetry' has echoed down most of this century.

War poetry emerged as a distinct genre with the soldier poets of the Western Front, providing ironic comment on the epic tradition, deploying satire, developing the devices of 'nature poetry' and the pathos of 'love poetry'. They had self-conscious successors in World War II. Numerous anthologies of war writing, even now, represent a moral peak in poetry, scaled also by writers confronting Auschwitz, the Irish Troubles, or, perhaps, responding to Bosnia. God, for most writers, no longer counts. In His/Her absence, war has again become the most august theme of verse, as it was for Homer. In the 1960s, Ted Hughes seemed more important than Larkin because he wrote about violence, while the latter harped on the miseries of diurnal surburban existence. I doubt if that criterion was sound. But whereas Larkin stupidly professed to despise foreign poets, Hughes was an internationalist, encouraging translations of European verse and himself translating the disturbing Yugoslav poet, Vasko Popa.

One of Hughes's last tasks before he died in 1998 was to translate six poems by Abdulah Sidran for Chris Agee's anthology *Scar on the Stone; Contemporary Poetry from Bosnia*. This impressive and very readable book gets several things right where they might have gone badly wrong. The translators include well-known poets – Charles Simic, Harry Clifton, Ruth Padel, Ken Smith, Kathleen Jamie –and distinguished scholars, Francis R Jones and Ammiel Alcalay. Agee has wisely compiled a selection of recent Bosnian poems – not just 'war poems' and 'anti-war poems' – only half of which were written after the break-up of Yugoslavia began in 1991. Most boldy, Agee recognises that poetry from an unfamiliar context cannot, or at least need not, "work single-handedly". He includes prose, some of it about Sarajevo during the years of siege by the poet Semezdin Mehmedinovic, who was there; impressive extracts from Miljenko Jergovic's collection *Sarajevo Marlboro*; 'before' and 'after' accounts of visits to the city by Francis R Jones and Agee himself, a fictionalised memoir from the death camps by Rezak Hukanovic and two striking pieces by distinguished dead outsiders. The great Serbo-Croat writer Danilo Kis (a Jew from Vojvodina, Yugoslavia's multi-ethnic northern province) wrote fiercely against nationalism in 1973, as "first and foremost paranoia". The Southern Irish essayist of Protestant background, Hubert Butler lived in the former Yugoslavia for three years in the 1930s, and wrote frequently about the country. In two pages from 1956, he distinguishes the geographically-based nationalism of the Young Ireland variety from the racism that gripped Europe after 1919, when "The old view that men should enjoy equal rights in the land of their birth began to seem hopelessly out of date". He quotes with sombre irony an Exiles' Charter published on behalf of 7.5 million Germans driven out of their homes in eastern Europe after Hitler's defeat in 1945. "God placed men in their homes." We should not forget (though most people have) that the recent European precedent for Serbian 'cleansing' in Croatia, Bosnia and Kosovo was the rape, murder and expulsion meted out to *Volksdeutscher* in places where their families had settled for centuries.

"Those to whom evil is done/ Do evil in return." – from Auden's 'Shield of Achilles' – is horribly apt. Serbians trace their Orthodox Christian state back to the 9th century. Defeat at Kosovo in 1389 by the Turks precluded the conversion of many Slavs to Islam and the total eclipse of the Serbian kingdom under Ottoman rule from the early 16th century. Serbia regained independence in 1878. In 1908, Austria's annexation of Bosnia-Herzegovina provoked a major international crisis. Two 'Balkan Wars' followed as the Turkish Empire crumbled, Kosovo was reconquered, then a Serbian assassin set off war throughout Europe by shooting the heir to the Austrian throne in Sarajevo. Serbians fought with the Western Allies against South Slavs in the Austro-Hungarian service. Post-war diplomacy united their country with Slovenia, Croatia, Bosnia, Montenegro and Macedonia, as 'Yugoslavia'. Orthodox Christians outnumbered northern Catholics; in the centre and south there were substantial Muslim minorities, Bosnian Slavs and non-Slavic Albanians, totalling 11.2 % in the 1931 census.

This unstable conglomeration suffered appallingly in 1941-5, when the Nazis occupied the whole country and created a puppet Croatian state under fascist leaders whose treatment of Serbs and others in concentration camps shocked even hardened SS men. The pattern of sectarian massacre and counter-massacre was occluded by the triumph of a secular, multi-ethnic guerilla movement under the leadership of Tito, a Croatian Communist. About 1,700,000 Yugoslavs died as a result of war from 1941-5, over a tenth of the population, many due to inter-ethnic fighting. Serbs in particular had scores against Croats. Just because they were paranoid, it did not mean that no-one had tried to get them. Serb spokesmen will declare that Albanians took over Serb land in Kosovo in the 1940s.

Yet in Sarajevo, Croats, Serbs and Muslims, lived peacefully side by side after 1945. The rate of intermarriage was the highest in the federation. When the government of Bosnia defied Serbian attempts to take over the whole of Yugoslavia in 1991, the new state resulting had no one distinctive religion, and almost all of its inhabitants spoke Serbo-Croat. Sarajevo stood for tolerance. Serbs remained there in solidarity with Muslim friends and neighbours against the sudden eruption of Serbian irredentism. Republican Spain in 1936-9 seemed to many outsiders to represent the battle of democracy against fascism. Chris Agee declares that "Bosnia was the Spanish Civil War of our time", as Sarajevo came to represent civil and multi-cultural values. Agee has sought poets who express "not the Chorus of identity, but the suppleness of the single sensibility".

Another thing Agee gets right is to begin with Mak Dizdar (1917-71), though he died two decades before the Bosnian War. Dizdar, from Herzegovina, fought in Tito's Resistance during World War II. His last and most important book is *Stone Sleeper* (1966). It is "rooted in the mystery of the schismatic Bosnian Church of the Middle Ages and its resistance to the heretic-killers of the established church – a mystery crucial to our understanding of modern Bosnia's strengths and tribulations".

Medieval Balkan dualism "saw mortals as fallen angels, expelled from heaven and imprisoned in human bodies. Nor did they return to heaven when they died, their souls stayed with their bodies until the Last Judgement". So their burial grounds, as in many cultures, have tremendous significance for the living. To 'cleanse' communities rooted for centuries, in such a perspective, becomes especially abhorrent. In a wonderful poem, 'Text about the hunt', Dizdar takes on the voice of Master Grubac, a 15th century tombstone sculptor buried in the necropolis on Boljuni, where in life he carved an elaborate hunting scene. This will remind us of Keats's 'Grecian Urn'. Its vision of life is equally poignant, more disturbing:

A tall horseman masters seething spaces of unrest
Handsome Dumb with deep desire Blind
without a sound he tramps behind
the baying and howling of hounds
panting thirsty straining for the blood of future
battlegrounds

Francis R Jones's English is wholly convincing. I am less convinced by the language of the three other poems, out of 15, which Jones translates with Middle English diction and spelling. The last poem he renders, 'A text about the five', dates from 1941 when the Nazis and their Croat Ustasa collaborators descended on Bosnia. To prevent their reading it, Dizdar wrote it out in the Arabic-based *alhamiya* script, to make it look like a religious text, since this had been the main script used for the Bosnian Slavic language throughout the Turkish occupation from early 15th to late 19th centuries. "One man counted bound and led/ One man whom the four men dread." A theme of *Scar on the Stone* is the threat perceived by others in Bosnia's *haeccitas*, its unorthodox and non-Orthodox differentness.

Differently, Abdulah Sidran has written screenplays for the brilliant Serbian film director Emir Kusturica's *Black Cat, White Cat* (1996). Two of the poems which Hughes translated with his usual effacement of his own verse personality in the interests of presenting a foreign writer, evoke violence from the past. 'Gavrilo' appropriates, sympathetically, the voice of Gavrilo Princep, assassin of the Austrian Archduke in 1914 – "Hurry, my heart, let's get the weapons". 'The Partisan Cemetery' recalls Tito's multi-ethnic, multi-cultural band of dourly committed heroes and heroines:

> . . . The dead
> Are here simply to set our sufferings
> In perspective. So now let's go – slowly
> After a feast, a wholly Slavonic
> Feast in a graveyard, souls intoxicated.
> Let the bone walk, the flesh
> Walk. The books, little sister, are open –
> The history is being written
> The Martyrology is open. What remains
> For us
> Is to remember our names, and never to forget them,
> Never, never again, to forget them.

Sarajevo's people weren't passive victims. They fought or supported fighters. This is neither a 'war' nor an 'anti-war' poem. Like Dizdar's evocation of long-dead heretics, it is poetry about history: a force in the present.

Izet Sarajlic (born 1930) was wounded by a shell in Sarajevo during the siege. Clearly an awkward customer, he became President of the Writer's Union of Bosnia-Herzegovina in 1971, was dismissed after 17 days and was later expelled from the Communist Party. But his clear, precise verse remained popular. His translators include Brodsky, Enzensberger and Yevtushenko – and, here, the Yugoslav-American poet Charles Simic. Sarajlic is one of the rare beings to make something out of Brechtian 'simplicity':

> If that Tuesday I had died in Berlin
> *Neues Deutschland* would announce that a Yugoslav
> writer of the middle generation
> suddenly died of a heart attack, while I – and this is
>   not just idle talk –
> need to croak on my native soil.
> You can see how good it is that I didn't die
>   and that I'm once again among you?
> You can whistle, you can applaud.
> You see how good it is that I didn't die,
> and that I'm once again among you all.

Again, this is not a 'war poem', but an incident in the ongoing relationship of a writer with his public, cherishable in its cocky understatement of feeling which might be called 'patriotic' but escapes its dodgier definitions.

Simic also translates Dara Sekulic, whom he compares with Emily Dickinson and Paul Celan. Agee himself, from cribs by Glavinic, renders the magnificent Marko Vesovic. 'White Hawthorn in Pape' says nothing about war, but presents themes of beauty and endurance in nature and human history. Ilija Ladin, translated by Ken Smith, is completely different, "highly influential among the 'rock' generation of poets of the eighties". Nuala Ní Dhomhnaill translates into both English and Irish Gaelic a poem by Ferida Durakovic, whose bookshop in Sarajevo was burnt down during the siege. It is called 'Georg Trakl on the Battlefield Revisited, 1993.'

> On high, above the planes, dwells God, the beloved
> eyes gleaming gold above the Sarajevo gloom.
> Fruit-blossom and mortar shells both fall beyond my window.
> Madness and me. Alone. We are alone. So alone.

Trakl (1887-1914) died young as a result of the First World War – he overdosed after a nervous breakdown in uniform on the Eastern Front – but cannot be called a 'war poet'. His last poems are the response of a remarkable Expressionist and Modernist poet to the horrors of war which extended his perception of the general crisis of bourgeois Europe. The aloneness evoked by Durakovic is a state of human consciousness which isn't confined to battlefield situations. The next poem by her ends with a cryptic reference to Edvard Munch – the poet's aloneness relates to Munch's famous peacetime image of *The Scream.*

My copy of *Scar on the Stone* now has pages inscribed "with love Vojka" and "Thanks for listening, Igor Klikovac". In April 1999 I heard them perform, with Chris Agee and Ken Smith at the Cúirt International Festival of Literature in Galway. Agee teased Vojka Djikic for her recklessness in front of the Irish traffic, not being used to left hand drive. She said, "I'd like to die here, in Galway". Later, she repeated that she wanted to die. Was this a joke? Her five poems in the anthology aren't directly about the siege. "We must bid farewell to the words/ which have betrayed us" is a statement of life passing – applicable anywhere. But clearly she is haunted by unhappy memories of the war. Igor, nearly four decades younger, got out of Sarajevo in 1993 and now works as a freelance writer in London. His four poems come directly from the Siege. A bag is packed for a 'trip' as the mortars thunder. A boy throws paper planes from a balcony as sirens wail, and the poet thinks of the "childlike absent-mindedness" on the faces of Serb killers. In a football stadium "The souls of the dead are taking the best seats". This handsome young man, striking new poet, may sustain his career in permanent exile. Will the siege have only a small role in his work, like that verse about Europe after D-Day written out of war service by Kingsley Amis? Or will nightmares haunt him as they did Robert Graves? The anthology title quotes a poem by Fahrudin Zilkic, 'Ricochet':

> It's when you hear the shot,
> and while you're lying flat on your
> face you're splattered with gravel.
> Ricochet –
> it's when a year later
> you recognise the scar on the stone
> where your life went on again.

Colin Mackay's extraordinary sequence of 68 poems, *Cold Night Lullaby*, presents an intersection between wartime Bosnia and everyday Edinburgh. It attracted press attention unusual for a 'slim volume' of verse, and a whiff of controversy. Did the events described 'really happen'? Except by those stupid enough to believe that poems only possess authority if they approximate to 'historical documents', the issue can be ignored as irrelevant. Like most vivid prose memoirs, Graves's *Goodbye to All That*, which we all think contains a 'truthful' account of the Western Front, has many passages of description and dialogue which must blend memory and imagination. Try writing down an account of any interesting experience immediately after it has happened, and you will discover that the process involves leaving out lots of remembered information for which there is too little space, and improvising other information on the basis of probability. The question we have to ask of writings of the kinds we call 'literary' is not 'are they exactly factual', but 'do they ring true?'

Mackay does ring true. His eloquent Foreword evokes the experience of someone inspired to drive from Edinburgh to Bosnia as an Aid Worker, part of the new "International Brigade without self-righteousness". Some of them died, and the death of a man whom he calls "Johnny" is the subject of an especially powerful poem. Johnny's real name, he suggests, was "Everyman", and Bosnia – both like Scotland and Napthali in the Bible, "lovely and a land lost in darkness" – was truly "Everywhere". Mackay's convoy reached a village, recently 'cleansed' by its Muslim inhabitants of Serbian families domiciled there for generations. One Serb woman had been allowed to remain, because her Muslim husband had died fighting for Bosnian independence. While Mackay was away in Sarajevo to arrange a flight out for Svetlana and her two children, Serbian fighters crossed the river and hit the village. "When we returned that afternoon, it was a place of corpses". Everyone had been killed. "Svetlana had been butchered. Ludmilla, six years old, was dead beside her with her brains blown out. Ahmad had disappeared". In the poem-sequence, Mackay discloses a passionate love affair with Svetlana. It has to be said that the lyricism of the poems which evoke this is not as convincing as the terseness of other sections:

> and my weaker half cried to you, Svetlana
> shield me, shield me
> between your serene breasts
> with the calm of your woman's strength,
> with the calm of your river
> and your village, its ancient hearth
> when day explodes around us
> in all the plains of the sun.

Earth Mother or Muse of all the Ages, she does not seem to belong with the vivid mundane entities of a war-torn land which Mackay presents elsewhere so well. "Serene breasts" is not quite a cliché, but it sounds like one. Yet in context this discrepancy is moving in itself – an attempt to assert the timeless against bad time. And the writing remains careful.

What is evident, and immensely impressive, throughout *Cold Night Lullaby*, is its effort towards precision. This is not 'protest poetry' pressing for a political reaction. It lives through as-if-observed detail. The details may not be patterned exactly as in this or that particular experience, but one feels that they derive from experience:

> In the burnt-out cafe
> stray pigs from a nearby farm feed
> on Ivan the chef and his two pretty waitresses.

> Somewhere
> the thud of mortars
> somewhere the splatter of shots,
> the screaming of an incoming shell,
> but beyond the blackened hole
> where the window used to be
> under the still-functioning Coca-Cola sign
> the pigs feed on.

The Coca-Cola sign is crucial to this passage. It verifies, so to speak, this implausible horror. The narrator, overpowered with hysteria, is given a jab by a medic and falls asleep to dream of Scotland, where:

> the office will be having its coffee break
> about now and the Number 27 bus
> will be halfway up Dundas Street
> and no one will believe that
> any of these things are happening
> in the same world as the office
> and the 27 bus.

The flat free verse is characteristic, though at times Mackay heightens or tightens his rhythms, or enriches his language. Poets should be wary of assuming that such verse, charged with powerful subject matter or thoughts, can thereby create durable poetry. But Mackay's successful use of it verifies horror as a more attention-seeking discourse couldn't. Again, that particular 27 bus enforces the important point that our everyday co-exists with horror. Mackay states fact. He does not say that people at home are morally deficient for not screaming about Bosnia all the time, merely that they can't imagine such things. Now, he can lift the verse towards a more 'poetic' conclusion, worked-for, earned, impressive:

> But the pigs are still feeding
> on Natasha's breasts and Ivan's buttocks
> done to a nicety and crisp around the edges,
> and the morning sky
> is blue as the robe of glory
> and warm as my love
> so glad to be alive
> to make these ashes speak.

'Love' . . . ? Proleptically, at this stage of the book, love of Svetlana? Or a wider love of humanity? The poem, 'Pigs', makes the macabre mundane, then turns back with bitter irony, but also warmth, to validate the burnt and eaten dead. So this is 'War Poetry', by a civilian, spanning like Graves's prose narrative from peace across war to haunted peace. More could be said about this remarkable book, and will be. To return to *The Heart of Europe,* in Agee's complex poem, 'Fleur-de-Lys', memories and talk of Bosnia tumble together with references to Ireland, to Achilles, to Moses in the bulrushes, to Herod, to the US Cavalry's massacre of Nez Perce Indians – "The same old story, males on the rampage".

We do not need to attribute the horrors of Bosnia (Rwanda, Algeria, Congo, Sierra Leone . . .) to some "Evil in the heart of humankind" in terms of traditional Christian theology and its doctrine of the Fall. From ancient times, males from puberty to young manhood have 'proved themselves' by aggressive behaviour. Young African or Melanesian warriors steal cattle or pigs, to provoke little wars of a ritual nature. In medieval Ireland a young chief had to establish his prowess by rustling. To be a man, the Bornean Dayak must bring home a head. The Capulets and Jets of Shakespeare's Verona and Bernstein's New York and the razor gangs of old Glasgow are instances of the same phenomenon as sends Hibs and Hearts supporters reeling through the streets of Edinburgh at weekends. Then they marry, have children, become peacable citizens. The murderous young males of Ireland over the last three decades have been given Causes by their elders' bigoted interpretations of history. The vast conscript armies of modern Europe have enlisted male violence and made its exercise respectable. The atrocities committed by Canadians in Somalia, part of a UN peacekeeping force, are a recent illicit example.

Prose fiction and drama, I'd suggest, can cope with this area of human experience when poetry, as a rule, can't – if it sets out in some old-fashioned way to be 'epic' it will alienate all decent readers. Contemporary verse commonly teases us to enter the undramatic persistences of life, the enigmas of unofficial personalities outside what Agee, as quoted before here, calls the 'Chorus of identity'. I think Harry Clifton's 'The Literal Version', in *In the Heart of Europe*, deals finely with the problem which we often have, not only with approaching a foreign poet in prose translation, but one of our own in a brand new book – "where is this guy at?":

> On Sundays at least, 'her lips' –
> I am quoting from various texts –
> 'Ice-cold, pressed against my cheeks'
> And his weekends, snowed in
> By a blizzard of football games
> On changing screens, or given over
> To cemetery visits, godlessness,
> Bleak honesty. For the dead
> Are everywhere – there has been war,
> There will be again . . .

That is the only reference to war in a lengthy poem about a Bosnian poet whose work, Clifton concludes, displays a "sense of solitude/ And a longing to connect". Connections are random, unpredictable. The German infantryman on the Eastern Front remembers Goethe as he moves in to destroy a village. The RAF bomber over Berlin suddenly recalls lines of Blake. After gang-rape, a Russian thinks of *Onegin*. The expansions of imagination and empathy and conscience which poetry provides are no guarantee against barbarous behaviour. But to keep writing verse in besieged Sarajevo was to affirm the faith that the connections which might be made could be worthwhile, and leave something behind to represent whatever oneself had been, or might have been.

Cold Night Lullaby, Colin Mackay, Chapman Publishing, £6.95; *In the Heart of Europe*, Amnesty International, Irish Section, Sean McBride House, 48 Fleet St, Dublin 2, Ireland, £5; *Scar on Stone: Contemporary Poetry from Bosnia*, ed. Chris Agee, Bloodaxe Books, £8.95

Le Tiers Monde: Naissance, Vie, Mort by John MacWilliam
The illustrations were featured in Red Ice by Colin Mackay, Mort as the cover.

Des Dillon

The Sorrow of the Glory

Monte Cassino. Walking the cloisters
in the vanishing steps of St Benedict;
in shattered fragments of pillars and stone
rebuilt from the ashes of war.
And stepping from the hot white
of the dusty cloisters the chapel's
exhaustless ornate gold construction
resurrects through the darkness
that is in my eyes because the light was too bright to see.

The simple story repaints itself
on the roof and the high dome
pointing to God. The painted Word falls
through the enormous ornament of church
and drifts on the melancholy voices of monks
chanting out the Sorrow of the Glory.

Somehow simple melodies laid live
over an imperceptible moan of organ
conjure more God than the bashful
of Angels and trumpet blowing alabaster boys.
This chapel is a loveletter to God.
The Words are curly metals and gold leaf plaster.
The sentences flat expanses of intricate marble.

There is no confusion that can't be fathomed
in the hush of foreign whispers,
the rush of shapes and colours
and the Word through an Italian microphone
crackling like little lightning bolts
off the hard unrelenting walls.

There is one light that shines always in the sanctuary
and a simple melody that laces clouds on my feet
and carries me at the head of the procession
of my life – I turn and looking back – oh
how many candles I have lit
from the one solitary light.

And so, blessed in the smoky breath
of incense I turn and walk out
into the light outside that blinds.

Stars At Arranmore

Suddenly, out of ambient streetlight
the stars are brighter; and that, with the sea
fuzzing flatbeds of sand like Galaxies
pressing on lonely rocks; I'm surrounded.
The Donegal lighthouse continues sweep
after sweeping. Alone, *I feel pick a star
that's me* – In here I'm out there. Over there
I'm silver rock lighthouse beam or streetlight

punctuating the Donegal shoreline.
I'm shining, is anybody watching?
The pristine glass sky – God's immaculate
conception – is vandal scraped by shooting
stars like nails on a brand new car. Is there
no-one watching? Is anyone listening?

I listen, but I can't make out
the waves drunken slurs and slurps
nor read the sad binary of stars
nor see correctly the melancholy
Morse of streetlights lamps and lighthouses.
The comfy foreign language of living room lights' speak.

But there's a light behind the sand dunes
as earth passes living room windows
of other galaxies and solar systems;
electromagnetic waves merge and part
on Messianic shores of deep space stars.
The earth *is* the question
out there, somewhere,
is the answer.

Glasgow Chamber Orchestra
(Concerto for Flute and Orchestra, Jaques Ibert [1890-1962])

The flute valves
opening and shutting,
clumping like little
frog mouths
among the songs of birds.

Through shoals of violins
twisting in the light
the Cello player swims
in and out
like a dolphin moving
in her own clear waters
free and blue.

Field of Willows

Des Dillon

It's this wee wummin an she's frantic. She's got a brown coat down to between her knees an her ankles. Brown boots wi fur inside them. An a hairnet. An there's this brown leather shoppin bag draggin her down so she walks tilt tilt tilt tilt like a brown penguin.

But there's nobody laughin. There's nothin funny. Her eyes are this way an that way. An they're blue her eyes. Really blue. Fear – that's what they're sayin to everythin they come to rest on before butterflyin off. Her body's sayin – wee wummin rushin through the Sauchiehall Street crowds to catch the Possil bus. But her eyes – they're sayin somethin different. They're sayin fear. The biggest fear. An the crowd that's partin to let her through can see their own biggest fear imprinted in her eyes. They move an they part an they glance back when she glances away.

I'm startin to hear what she's sayin cos this reporter's got a microphone shoved in her face. The telly must've been there interviewin people at the January sales or somethin. She passes into where the camera must be an it swings an keeps its monstrous silver eye on her. It doesn't blink or look away. It follows the wummin an the reporter jostlin through the outskirts of the crowd.

The crowd's quite a cosmic thing. It's like a star's exploded an flung all its debris out. Sauchiehall Street's the cosmos. There's a smatterin of people on the edges but as they go in they get tighter until they're coagulated on the rim of what must be a black hole. Gravity.

An that's where she's goin. The wee wummin wi the tilt tilt walk. She's bumpin her way towards the black hole. Her own personal fear's takin her to her own black hole. She'll be sucked in an disintegrated. She was only out to buy some pies wi her man. He decided to look in A T Mays while she was in the shop. She's still movin tilt tilt an steady through the grippin crowd. It's when she reaches the critical lip an bursts through into the vortex I hears what she's sayin.

Is ma man hurtit?

Silence.

A cough an the shuffle of feet.

A gust of wind.

A distant siren.

Is ma man hurtit?

But there's nobody answers. There's just the reporter an his microphone hissin like a snake between the words. An the people in the crowd can't answer her eyes. She's grabbin them by the shoulders an shakin them.

Is ma man hurtit for Godsakes?

But they still won't answer. Next thing she slumps down to her man crumpled on the slabs. Stabbed to death by a junkie for a fiver. She's sayin his name,

Alistair! Alistair!

But it's not to him she's sayin it. She's on her knees like she's prayin wi the rain drippin onto her palms and she's sayin his name to the crowd. Like they can bring him back. There's blood on her hands now. Blood an water. She stretches them up to the sky an wails. The circle she's kneelin in could be a spotlight on any stage. It's as well bein a rock in deep space cos no human communication could comfort her.

The newsreader moves onto – and now for the sport – Celtic are sure to beat Rangers tomorrow, he says. A certainty. That's where his money's goin anyhow.

It's the West End. The party's mobbed with snobs. Lawyers, Doctors an Civil Engineers. It's at the smoothin down of frocks an dippin for nuts in fancy crystal stage. News at Ten's on. The door opens an some important people come in like horses out the frost. Snowflakes are fallin in droves past the window an the fire's on. Real flame gas job. Cosy. It's all shakin jackets an kissin cheeks.

The Scottish news comes on.

Watch this! I go to the blonde wi the red lips. There's somethin different about this report. Like when I seen *Braveheart*. There was somethin different about the feelin in the pictures. It catches everyone's attention gradually. There's only glasses clinkin an fags gettin sparked up. The whole party follow the same wee wummin to the same places I followed her to on the six o'clock news.

After the wummin goes, Is ma man hurtit! There's this silence. I looks round expectin sympathy.

Is ma man hurtit! Goes the blonde through her nose – Well! Talk about giving Glasgow a bad name? Really. Is ma man huuuurtit!

There's another pause. The snow's still whisperin it's edges off the glass. Then the party exploded in super nova laughter.

When it's died down this young Lawyer says Field of willows, that's what it means.

Eh? says his bird.

Field of willows – Sauchiehall Street – that's what it means. Gaelic.

Iiiiiiis iiiiiiit? She goes in these long vowels that only out an out snobs an teenage schoolgirls use.

An all night long there's parodies of Is ma man hurtit creatin laughter throughout the rooms an lobbies of the flat. Every now an then I could hear the lawyer tellin some short skirt that Sauchiehall Street is The Field of Willows.

Letters From a Well-Wisher

Helen Lamb

Dear B

You don't know me but I have been assigned to observe you – your habits, movements and so on.

And I'm not happy with what I see – The Bricksworth Building Society Monday to Friday, your slow unwinding Saturday, sprawling Sunday – then like some jealous slob of a god, you survey Football Italia and see that it is good.

In the past few weeks, I've learned so much about you, B, more than you will ever know. And yet CONTROL forbids me to pass my findings on, not even a hint as to where you might be going wrong. I'm sorry but I don't agree with this policy of non-interference. Somebody has to tell you. You need to be told.

It wouldn't be so bad if you actually built something. But where are the bricks? How are you supposed to start? Take my advice, B, get some today. Also, may I suggest, a trowel and cement.

Yours constructively

A Well-Wisher

Dear B

Do you remember A, your fearless childhood friend? He was my first case-study. A was some kid, wasn't he? Always tumbling out of trees and playing chicken in the traffic. His injuries were spectacular. Not just the usual collection of skinned knees. He got concussion and compound fractures. And then there was the putting flag he speared through his left foot. The tooth embedded in his shin. Luckily, not yours. Though, at the time, you wished it was. Because you envied him, didn't you, B?

You stole plasters from the First Aid Box and stuck them where they showed. But no one ever asked what you'd been up to. A always had a gorier story. He was just that kind of boy.

I say *was* – because A's not with us anymore, not since the poaching expedition. Remember? You were there as well. But A went over first and when the owner let the rottweilers loose, you hid behind the wall. You couldn't bear to watch. But you still heard him, his feet pounding faster and faster and your heart raced with him, very nearly gave out too before the dogs caught up with him. You almost died yourself that day.

And A didn't call on you. Not anymore. Though, now and then, you thought you heard him, times out riding your bike when he even got quite loud.

LOOK NO HANDS

LOOK NO HANDS

Of course, you were too sensible to listen to a ghost. You ignored him. You kept on ignoring him, B. So he asked me to pass on this message for him. Don't forget to have fun – he says. That's all.

A Well-Wisher.

Dear B

I was watching you at the check-out queue in Tesco's the other day and your trolley saddened me. The lack of taste, the poverty of imagination it displayed. You're not so hard up. You don't need to eat spaghetti hoops every day. Six cans – I counted. And one of ravioli. Anything for a change, I suppose. But that solitary can looked like a cry for help to me. Ravioli is desperate stuff.

And Cheddar cheese is for mice. Are you a mouse or a man? Try Parmesan and *real* spaghetti. Or something blue – a Stilton or a nice ripe Brie. It's not as dangerous as it looks. You'll survive. Think about it, B, between now and next shopping day. Think about Parmesan.

A Well-Wisher.

Dear B

Is your door locked and bolted? Are your windows secured? Is your little home fully insured against fire, theft, accident and sundry Acts of God? Lightning? Locusts? Earthquake? Flood? Have you saved up for that rainy day? I bet you have.

But do you sleep easier? I don't think you do. I've seen your light. At two and three o'clock in the morning, it flickers on and your flame curtains glow. Your bed is restless, your bed is on fire. Or that's how it looks from the outside. That's how it looks to me. I could be wrong.

Maybe a burglar broke into your dream. Or, sensing my presence, you woke with a start and decided to get up and check the small print on your policies. Are you covered for well-wishers? Do you have any protection against optimists like me?

Because I do have hopes for you, dear B. The insomnia, for example. That gives me hope. That is an excellent sign. And those lumps in your mattress, do you know what they are?

Possibilities.

Disturbing possibilities. Felicity from accounts is one. Office hours, you ignore her. But at night, you can't avoid her. Her breasts hump the bed. You toss. You turn. Her knee digs into the small of your back.

Don't ask me how I know these things. Let's just say I'm the sensitive type. And I'm telling you, B, Felicity is a distinct possibility.

A Well-Wisher.

Dear B

You've been tearing up my letters. Don't think that I don't know. All my helpful hints reduced to useless scraps of paper.

I have written. I have written. I've put in for a transfer but until CONTROL gets back to me it looks like I am stuck.

My life is not my own. And yours is getting me down. If you were a half-decent host, it wouldn't be so bad. If you made some effort to entertain. But I don't even get to see your friends. You do still have some, don't you, B? If not, I thought we could invite Felicity round for dinner tonight. Don't worry, I can be discreet. She won't even know I'm here.

A Well-Wisher.

Dear B

Just a quick note to let you know I'll be away for a few days. Orders from CONTROL. I'm getting too close to the subject. That's you, by the way. The subject. And what a boring one you are. You didn't ask her, did you? No. You didn't even say good morning.

AWW

Arbroath

Dear B – Hope you like the postcard of the Deil's Head (see over). You wouldn't wish to be here but it would do you good to stand on the edge of these windy cliffs. The erosion of sandstone is treacherous and quick. Where your toes curl today may be the void tomorrow. Or sooner. Who knows? Who can predict when the ground will give way?

AWW

Dear B

Got back lunchtime yesterday and resumed my tail at once. Though I don't suppose you noticed. The extra shiver in the breeze? The slanted shadow that fell from nowhere? That was me. And twice we touched. We were that close.

So here I am. Again. I did enjoy the break but the comforts of the B&B had begun to pall and I confess I missed my vigil. Couldn't help worrying while I was away. And not without good reason it would seem.

I know I'm not supposed to write. CONTROL would not approve. And, I admit, I was the one who wanted more excitement. All the same, it's one thing to take a calculated risk, quite another to wreak havoc on the public highway. Yesterday evening on the way home from work, you jumped the lights five times. And all this doubling back on your tracks is downright anti-social in a one-way system.

Illustration by David Stephenson

Trust me. Nobody is following you. I would know. I keep a very close eye on you. So clunk-click for now and drive carefully.

A Well-Wisher.

Dear B

I don't think you've met C. A fascinating character. Dangerously erratic on the road. And unreliable. I never know what he'll decide to do next. Will he/won't he grace the Bricksworth with his presence today?

We'll just have to wait and see. But first there's something you should know.

The thing is, B – he looks a lot like you. And some of your less discerning colleagues have trouble telling you apart. Felicity sure notices the difference though, can't take her eyes off you. Sorry– I meant *him*. Just a slip of the pen, but now that I pause to consider it, fortuitous perhaps. For it suddenly occurs to me, B, what with the resemblance and everything, if you were to impersonate him . . . ?

A Well-Wisher.

Dear B

It is with deep regret that I write to inform you this will be my last letter. CONTROL says it's got to stop, and, as of 1400 hours today, I've been relieved of my responsibilities.

So, B, you're on your own from now on. Wish the same could be said for me. At this very moment as I force my pen across this final page, a hefty sour-breathed gentleman stands guard at my shoulder. Someone to watch over me. I think that's how CONTROL put it. And what is the charge? What did I do to deserve this foul fate?

Disruptive influence, apparently. They tell me you will never be the same again, B. Can't say I'm very sorry about that.

My jailer's shaking his head. He heaves another punishing smelly sigh. If I would just show some remorse – he says. This attitude will get me nowhere.

Of course, I fought the decision. You know me. Don't you, B? You know me?

CONTROL tells me you don't want to. *You* are the one who got me locked away. You shopped me, B. Is that true? Perhaps you're more devious than I thought. But no-one can keep me inside forever. Not even you. One day, I'll be out of here. With good behaviour, my jailer says, who knows . . ? When he speaks I'm obliged to hold my breath, but the reek of his righteousness still gets up my nose. He says he might even be prepared to recommend me for parole. Not if I break out first he won't.

Expect me soon, B – with a vengeance. I will be back.

A Well-Wisher.

Tom Pow

The Battle for the Atlantic

Parked cars hunched up on scrub
first drew us, then the worn track
led through the heat, past brick

catacombs with their small
dark secrets, to the roll
of the endless Atlantic.

Sails turned like butterfly wings.
The cliff rolled like a ribbon
below us; the track a hem

through purple clumps of heather.
We passed other tourists,
cameras bobbing on their chests,

as if they bore something
that we risked bringing back.
Our destination was a rock

carved into a fortress
with a house, a hangar, a row
of broken billets. A stone's throw

of a bridge between knuckles
of rock moored it like a prison ship
off-shore, where it caught the drift

of all eyes along the clean
lines of the coast. Turn the world
on its head: this rock's a cloud

no light can penetrate;
an element that cannot meld.
All the tourists who cavort

on its back look out of place:
they are dancing on a grave.
Yet there were nights we drove

into the little fishing towns
with their bunting, and bars
almost jaunty with the sounds

of a seafaring song;
and, as our pastis *clouded,*
we laughed; and forgot the drowned

and the lost, each with its shadows
of grief stretching away
into the darkness. Driving back

from the counterfeit towns,
the waters silvery now,
though that base rock still crow-

black and apart, I thought
how evil sits in your heart
like a fist or a cancer

that somehow anchors
itself to you and shadows
your rude and sunny health.

So this rock casts its own light
and draws us like a magnet.

On Hearing of your Illness

So how did it happen? Twenty five years
of friendship – not one minute of it
on foreign soil (and no love letter
till this). The closest we came, the past

glorious summer in the west. We lived it
without doors at Ravenstone, surrounded
by sycamore and beech so richly green
not a breath of wind touched us; the corn

ripened at our backs beneath a sun
that made each day its predicate. We drove
one afternoon to a beach on the Mull,
down hot little roads slashed by sunlight

and shadows, to find a white eiderdown
of mist had rolled over the Irish Sea.
I picnicked in the moony sun, digging
my heels into the sand, while I watched you

wade into the mist, poised as if you bore
a clay pot on your head through heat and dust;
and emerge from it too as if time hadn't
touched you in all those years, your body

a companion piece to your teenage son's.
You waved then to a world composing itself
in those brown otter-bright eyes. That summer
anyone with a boat pulled mackerel

from the glassy bay. Freezers were stacked
with them, yet each day brought fresh offers.
On my last night at Ravenstone, we cooked
the petrol shiny fish on a wood fire,

the flesh so white, so fresh it fairly crumbled
in your hands. We shared a grassy mound,
a rowdy crowd of renegades, our air
suffused with sweet smells of woodsmoke

and marijuana. It was, let's say,
Wigtownshire exotic! Some months later
I heard of the phosphorus bombs raked
from Beaufort's Dyke: 4,000 fire-sticks,

caked with decades of rust that littered
these pilgrim shores. And I recalled a slight
unsteadiness as you'd waved from the sea's edge,
before that clouded landscape took you to its heart.

West Cork Coastline

You can take any number
of twisting single track roads
down to the coast. We did: roads

that wind between a bothy's
scrubbed steps and hen coops so close
you can see the copper chests

brush the muddy dark aside.
Roads that seem on the point of
giving themselves up for lost

where the livings once did
and a fresh harled settler's house –
blue dingy tipped on the lawn –

stands at the ruined thresholds
of famine. Past such a dead
township, over a field starred

with thistles, to the cliff's edge –
from where you squint along
a runway of fishermen's buoys

to the bay you want, cupping
its grail of blue water. So you ask
how it is again you've landed

at Prisoner's Cove
not knowing how it was named
or whose is the shadow haunts

the dark cottage curtained
with blankets and lays out food
for the angular black cat

and her three mewling kittens.
Still you're not disheartened:
the 'slipway' stones are shaped

by the roughest tides; they skim
the still water like fish scales
out where you want to go next –

between furnace walls
of fuschia, bindweed white hot
in the late afternoon sun.

One last field of thistles
and from the foot of a cliff
an explosion of children

detonates the still landscape.
Four or five, and a dog, charge
into the water with bright

mercuric sparks before
some music you are deaf to
calls them, all flailing limbs, back

into the rock face. Again.
And again till you realise
that there is the place you've sought

all along – on the wrong side
of the bay and with no road
you can see to take you there.

Yet the satisfaction you feel
in their laughter, or else in
the laughter whose silvered notes

don't reach you across the bay's
blue vestments, suggests to you
today's search is at an end.

Mr McArthur

The rogue sheep on its knees nudges
a bony head at the kettle
of milk on my lap. I hold both
handle and lid with canny conceit,
for the kettle's tin sides
are in the broad grip of our host,

Mr McArthur himself, whose arm
brushes my cheek with sweet
smells of straw and milk.
                              Each evening
he places the white jug of milk,
straight from the cow, beside butter
and jam. And for a moment
stands in the door, a large-boned, florid
featured man, whose bottom teeth jut
over toothless gums. Our mother smiles
with a "That will be fine. Thank you,"
and a shoulder-straightening that says,
No childish words please – on the still
steaming milk, its surface jewelled
with golden gobs of fat.
                              The oiled coat
of the sheep brushes my knees
and I curl my fingers away
from the desperate, milk-whiskered mouth.
What a useless little bugger
I am! Seven years old, I let slip
two faded floral cups, then
watch Mr McArthur bearing
the pieces away like petals
in his raw hands. A gate's spar cracks
when I swing on it; a door's slat –
I swear – caves in before the wind.
But Mr McArthur simply
smiles, or tuts, as if nothing
is worth anything, or as if
the landscape of wind, rain and sea
is too fluid for the tight space
of apology we'd pen him in.

Saying goodbye, in that boxed hall
with the new-mended door, I sense
the generous presence of his life;
the routine acts he's opened up
to me. How have I repaid him?
We have no language but this
clumsy disclosing of ourselves.
My tears are black on the stone flags.
I know they are no apology,
but in the stiff silence, *sorry's*
not what I want to say most.

Landscapes

There is a time in life when you just take a walk:
And you walk into your own landscape.

from *Sketchbook 1:* Willem de Kooning – 1904-1997

1.

Dense rhododendron bushes almost mask
the start of the track. Oak boughs cast

shadows on sunlit days across it. Ferns
grow unchecked. Once milk churns

and linen passed by to the Big House
and, halfway along, a walled garden still shows

raspberries like spinning tops. The iron door
lies open. Within these walls, desire

rises in you like sap. The world pounds
with green fire: *find me*, you pray, *find me.*

2.

Ferns break apart on your shins and thighs;
sand runs so quickly through your toes,

it tells of no time but this instant,
on a helter-skelter, cool, green-tented

path to the sea. As if it were red hot rock,
you take the crumbly seaweed; lock, stock

and barrel, leap driftwood and the clear mines
of jellyfish (for once with no questions) –

till the cold brine takes you and expels you
and teaches you all the body's truths anew.

Illustration by Hugh Bryden

3.

The air is smoky with an early haar
as your father, hen basket in hand,

strides up the hill to a suburban
country track, where he stoops over such rare

dandelion heads, at their milky fullest,
their leaves fall from them in long green straps.

For your white rabbits, the best of the crop.
And how fresh is his gift! Lightly pressed

in the basket, greenness unfurls:
on taut skin, you stencil a string of pearls.

4.

One after another, they fall from his hand
onto the ground; and, as we look, the only sound

is of paper brushing paper like a beat,
each beat equal to the eye. They are Light,

Colour and Movement – seaweedy, swampy; or fields
in the early morning, tinder dry, but folded

under haze. At first they are unnamed,
his hand drawing them from the landscape of his mind.

The best are like staring into a busy pond.
You can stay with one longer by raising your hand.

Illustration by Hugh Bryden

11.

When the giant hillside beech was torn down
by its own weight, or weight of the storm it found

more malleable than it, it lay raw and wounded,
its stars of roots and the earth laid bare. A loom

of well-worn tracks became useless; the mulch
of the forest was bruised, dug into, till the pulse

of the shock, it seemed, slowed and once more growth,
nimble rooted, asserted itself. Tall foxgloves

flourish now in the shade of the trunk, and ferns,
lock onto sunlight with hungry green thorns.

12.

These thick old webs are patternless, anarchic.
One holds a louse like a water beetle

swimming to no-surface. A moth sticks
to the glass like a seed head leaked

from the outside; a world that's level with it –
of light shredded by nettles with dark

leathery leaves and purple stems. Pebble chip
spiders on threadlike legs work

secretly here. The crimson woundwort suggests
each flower is an extravagance, a hooded dress.

Illustration by Hugh Bryden

The Nine O'Clock Vampire

Frances Campbell

The fight started the minute Marie rang the doorbell. Children's voices.

"You get it!"

"Naw, you get it!"

"Shut up and get it will you – I'm watching TV."

Then the mother's voice intervened. "How can you no get it, you?" It sounded as if she had come through from the kitchen. Marie heard a whack.

"Ah, leave off!"

All the time the footsteps were approaching the door. It opened. "Yes?" The mother stood there, her face criss-crossed with temper. Marie held out her ID card: "Hello, I'm from the Universal Market Research Agency. Would you mind answering some questions?" She stole a glance into the living room. A boy of fifteen lay on the floor guarding the channel changer like a dog with a bone. A younger boy was concentrating on his toys. The mother breathed in audibly: "Look, I'm just in from work and I've the tea to get on. Do you mind? Goodnight". She was already closing the door.

"Sorry to trouble you," Marie's voice sang with relief. She didn't want to go in anyway – but once she had rung, she was obliged to go through her spiel.

Normally, it was happy people who asked her in. Like the woman last week who had won a cruise at the bingo. Marie smiled as she walked up the next path. The bingo woman had tried to answer the questions thoughtfully but her excitement kept bubbling through – she was going to take her mother; and it was a bingo cruise so they could play as they sailed round the islands. Her man was staying home so she would stock the freezer with casseroles.

At the next house the woman who answered was chewing a mouthful of food. "Sorry, we're eating," she smiled.

Men on their own often asked Marie in while they were eating but women never did. It was funny the differences. The people who invited her in could be categorised. They included:

Old people (lonely)

People off sick

Shift workers (bored)

People hoping for freebies

Fellow workers who appreciate you have a job to do

People who think market research is a necessary science

People who don't know how to say no

Opinionated farts and

People who feel sorry for you

Once, she had even been taken in for revenge. It was a husband and wife. She had heard them shouting before she rang but she was behind on her target and only got paid for interviews, not ringing bells. The wife came to the door, high-coloured and angry. He stood behind her, halfway down a corridor.

"I'm conducting a survey for the Universal Market Research Agency." Marie glanced down the corridor, "but . . . actually, it's men I need to interview."

The woman's eyes glinted. Her mouth pursed as though tasting a new flavour. "Aye, he'll do it. Come in." She tossed her head and let Marie in.

Marie perched on the edge of their couch and called up the questionnaire on her computer. She interrogated the man about his choice of shaving cartridges, whether he bought shirts with co-ordinated ties, and the qualities he looked for in socks. It took an hour and by the time she left she had, at least, united the couple in that she was now the common enemy.

She opened yet another garden gate and walked up the path. It was the dead hour – tea time. It fell at different times depending on the locality and was especially bleak in poor schemes and high flats. But this street was fine – established properties; owned with a mortgage; skilled workers and retired. She was in a mature garden lit by long slivers of light from the cracks where the curtains joined.

She stood outside the storm doors and rang the bell. No one answered. Realising no one would come, she waited, making it her own garden for a while. The night was damp and as she breathed in she smelled the earth and the soft, swollen bark of the trees. She felt like a cat out smelling the night. It was an outdoor job, really, despite the hours spent on sofas. She had driven thirty miles to reach this town. Before today she had only heard its name on the News – in connection with murders or factory closures. But now she had been in its houses, in the lives of its people. Six people so far. Her target was eight.

At the next door a man gave her a wide smile.

"Hello, I'm from the Universal Market Research Agency, we're conducting a survey . . ."

"Aagh!" He stepped back, crossing his arms as if to ward off a vampire. Marie laughed and he brought his arms down to reveal laughing eyes.

"Message received." She shook her head as she went down the path; time was running out. She was only allowed to work till nine o'clock but she needed two more victims or she wouldn't make a living wage. She sighed. Who cared? Who gave a toss about her earning power? No one. Her husband was an accountant, for Christ's sake. What she earned in a day, he could make in an hour. The economics of it didn't bear looking at. But if she hit her target at least she could hold her head up in the knowledge that she wasn't her husband's parasite.

Another door.

"Sorry, I'm on the phone." A middle-aged man cradled the receiver with one hand and barred the door with the other.

Marie nodded and turned back towards the gate. But as her fingers felt the cold iron of the latch a voice called: "Stop!"

She looked round. A boy was in the doorway, pushing the phone-man aside and leaping down the steps.

"Wait! I'll do your interview. I'm a marketing student. I want to see how it works."

He led her inside. He was about nineteen, dark, with a friendly effusiveness that made her wonder if he might be gay.

"My name's Paul," he said, settling her on an easy chair then sitting on the floor like a child before its teacher.

She switched on her laptop and looked at him. "Why don't you sit at my side and watch the screen?" Professionally, it was bad practice but nobody had ever run down the path after her and she wanted to give something back.

The first section focused on nasal sprays:

<<Which of these brands of decongestant have you seen advertising for in the last 3 days?>>

The man on the phone hung up and walked past them to the kitchen. Marie heard him talking with a woman and, soon after, the sound of knives and forks on plates.

"Aren't you eating with your parents?"

"I'm a vegetarian. I make my own."

"Ah."

There followed sections on greeting cards, insurance, fast food and banks. By the end Paul had stopped watching the screen. He was staring at his shoes and answering in a monotone. Marie felt gratified – even he was bored. Most people were. The whole business was a con. She was taught to say: "Can I ask some questions" – and never to volunteer that it might take an hour. She was colluding in stealing people's time.

Her attention returned to Paul. "I need some details now. Who is the chief earner in the household, please?" She dropped her voice, anxious that his parents might hear. Paul hesitated then dropped his voice as well. "My Dad. Mum's only part-time."

"And what does your father do for a living?"

"He's a director of a construction firm."

"How many employees is he responsible for?"

Paul shrugged. "About twenty. I thought this was my interview?" He looked at the screen again. It read:

Please code social class. Choose option:

A	C2
B	D
C1	E

Marie pressed 'B' and explained: "I have to class your father because his salary reflects the spending power of the household. It's the same for me. On my own I'd be a 'C1'. But because of my husband I'm classed as a 'B'." He looked at her. "Don't you have another job? Do you do this full time?"

"It's all anyone has offered me. I've been out of things so long . . . Raising kids," she shrugged. "You're right, it's a shit job. I should be doing something better." She shut her computer and leant on the top like a desk. "It's a funny thing about marketing – at the top it's glamorous, dynamic. But out in the field, you're a social pariah."

Paul shifted uncomfortably: "Why are you doing it then?"

The kitchen door opened and his father re-appeared.

"I'm don't know. Sometimes it doesn't make much sense."

It was eight o'clock when she stepped back outside. She would knock doors for another fifteen minutes then call it a night. It had been dark for hours. Not that the dark scared her. The whole business of going into people's homes was risky. Like the money issue, it didn't bear thinking about. But her own right hand betrayed her; every time she dressed for work it selected the best pair of knickers from her drawer. In case she got raped. She had an irrational fear of seeing her shabbiest knickers held up in court. Irrational? Well, maybe not – she was in control of the knicker situation, if not of the chances of sexual attack. Her first preference was white – hip hugging cotton with lycra but not too high cut.

Eight ten. She was in a block of private flats. A group of men on their way out had allowed her to bypass the entry system. She climbed up to the third floor and rang the bell of the flat nearest the stairs. In a moment a shuffling could be heard. The door opened and a woman appeared. She was in her late fifties and clasping her cardigan with two hands like a shawl. Her face had deep shadows sunk in coarse skin. Marie thought she might be ill.

"Hello, I'm conducting a survey . . ."

The woman shook her head. "I don't live here. There's no point asking me."

"Oh . . . is the householder in?"

"Miss Gray died four months ago."

"I'm sorry. Were you related?"

"I looked after her . . . I took care of her for fifteen years."

"So you do live here?" Marie was confused.

"Yes, but I have to move out next week."

"Well, if you live here we can do an interview."

The woman stepped back: "I suppose you'd better come in."

Marie followed her down the hall. Had she been disgustingly pushy? The woman was bereaved . . . But that was four months ago.

They went into a wide, modern living room and the woman turned in the middle of the floor. "I don't know what use I'll be. I'm too old. And I don't go out much now."

"But I have specific orders to interview women in your age group. My company wants to know what you think."

"Really?" the woman's head tilted. "Would you like a cup of tea?"

"Mmmm. Do you mind if I take my coat off?"

"No, sit down. The furniture is all Miss Gray's. It's going to auction next week."

Marie looked round. Most of the pieces were antique. Upholstered in tapestry – an armchair with footstool to match, a chaise-lounge with sensuous, wooden curves. The carpet was red, the walls rag-rolled a striking yellow. The decor spoke of a much stronger personality than the woman who had opened the door.

The woman brought back the tea. Marie unwrapped the foil from a biscuit and handed the woman a prompt card. "Could you look at this list of newspapers and tell me which you read, if any?"

The Times	*The Scotsman*
The Telegraph	*The Herald*
The Guardian	Local Daily
The Independent	

"Just *The Times*," said the woman.

"*The Evening Times?*"

The woman nodded and Marie keyed in 'Local daily'.

A section on TV viewing came next then Marie handed the woman another card: "This section is about environmental services. Could you tell me which of the following you would give priority?"

The woman studied the card.

> Graffiti
>
> Dog toilets
>
> Grass cutting
>
> Recycling

She considered for a few moments then said: "Recycling". She was sitting up straighter. Marie shifted about giving her own spine some exercise. She handed over another card. "Which of the following do you think the council should prioritise?"

> New house building
>
> Upgrading of property
>
> Council house sales

"I think there's enough house building," the woman drew a line of cessation in the air with her hand. "It eats up all the countryside. Do you know what I saw the other night out the back?"

"What?"

"A fox. A beautiful creature."

Marie smiled and ventured a question that wasn't on her machine. "Do you have any pets?"

"No, Miss Gray wouldn't have any. She couldn't abide dogs. She was that frail, you see, she was frightened they would knock her over."

"How old was she?"

"Seventy-five. But she was never well. I did everything for her. Shopping. Cooking. Cleaning. For fifteen years. I thought she'd leave me the house, you see. But she left it to charity and the furniture too. I didn't get a stick."

"And did she say she'd leave the house to you?"

"Not in so many words. But it was always understood. It hurts, you know – caring for her all these years and now it's as though I never mattered at all. I don't understand why. That's what I can't get out of my mind." The woman's posture had sunk again.

"Have you somewhere to live?" Marie forgot she was there to interview. The woman sniffed. "The council have given me a flat. But there's nothing in it – no cooker, no bed."

"What about the Red Cross? They help with things like that."

"The man who's taking Miss Gray's furniture said he'd find me something. He can't let me have any of this because it's too valuable."

Marie pictured a flat full of the solid, anaesthetic remnants of the fifties. Square, heavy table. Dutiful couch. Carpets that were matted and dull. It was the kind of furniture young people started out with – students and girls who got pregnant too soon.

"You know," she said, "Miss Gray has treated you badly. But you have one thing she hasn't – Life! She's pushing up daisies and look at you, you've another twenty, thirty years in you. You have a flat. And, who knows, you could get a dog." Marie was growing excited.

The woman's eyes were alight as well. She looked more like what she was – a robust, intelligent woman well into her middle years.

Marie laughed: "I can see you striding round the streets with your dog. And there's so many things to become involved in – you're obviously bright. People will snap you up for committees and charity work. Environmental stuff, animal rights – you name it." Marie was waving her hand.

"You think so?" The woman's voice was hopeful, her expression light, bemused, entertained.

"Of course – look at me. I should have had an inheritance too. But my father left everything to my brother. Just because I was married, he thought my husband should provide. But I need to earn my own living – you can't rely on other folk."

The woman had stopped listening and was thinking her own thoughts. "I could get a dog. Maybe I could get one at the pound."

"Attagirl!" Marie clapped her computer. "Listen, I just need some details. And do you mind if I use your loo before I go?"

In the car, Marie switched on the heater and, as soon as she stopped shivering, filled in her quota sheet. She'd hit her target although that last interview meant she was running late. Still, she was glad she had taken her time with the woman. It had helped confirm in her own mind why she couldn't be a stay-at-home wife; it would make her feel too insecure.

In the back of the car she kept a flask and some food. Chocolate and a buttered roll. With steamy, black coffee. She switched on the radio. It was playing something old and melodic. Outside, the street was dark and quiet, the foliage on the trees swaying in the light from a street lamp. It was her patch. They were her people. Funny, how she took ownership of everywhere she'd been. She travelled round the country gathering knowledge of people and territory. She smiled. It was a fanciful way of looking at how she earned her living. Easier to do at the end of the day than the start.

John MacWilliam

Dùghall Bochanan

La a' Bhreitheanais/ The Day o Judgment

'N sin fàsaidh rudhadh anns an speur,
Mar fhàir na maidne 'g èirigh dearg,
Ag innse gu bheil Iosa fèin,
A' teachd 'na dhéigh le latha garbh.

Grad fhosglaidh as a chéil' na neòil,
Mar dhorus seòmair an àrd Rìgh,
Is foillsichear am Breitheamh mòr,
Le glòir is greadhnachas gun chrìch.

Tha 'm bogha-frois mu'n cuairt d'a cheann,
'S mar thuil nan gleann tha fuaim a ghuth;
'S mar dhealanach tha sealladh shùl,
A' spùtadh as na neulaibh tiugh.

A ghrian, àrd-lòcharan nan speur,
Do ghlòir a phearsa gèillidh grad;
An dealradh drillseach thig o ghnùis,
A solus mùchaidh e air fad.

A reid lowe leamin in the heivens,
Skire as the dawn that burns up nicht,
Annoonces Christ, and wi him tae,
His last Day's fearsome licht.

The cloods are speldit like a door
Tae the chaumer o the King, an there
The Justice General kythes himsel,
In glory cled for ivermair.

The gow o licht is roun his heid,
His thrapple bullers like glens in spate.
His glower skites doun like fireflaucht
Frae heiven's black weet sclate.

The sun, heich lantren o the lift,
Blinters an fades forenent his bleeze.
Afore the brichtness o his face
It dwines an dees.

As it pits on its murnin claes,
Skailt bluid sall be upon the mune,
The energies o space be shuik
An aw the starns cawed doun.

Like fruits spanghewit tae the lift
Frae blastit brainches strippit clean,
They shouer doun like rainfaw; –
Blearit their licht as deid men's een.

He rides his cheriot o fire
An aw aroun the thunners thudder,
Rairin oot-throu the universe,
Teirin the cloods wi whap and whudder.

His ragin wrath lunts shuits o flame
That frae his cheriot wheels ootspreid
An flude the warld an wap it roun
Wi seas o burnin reid.

The elements will melt an rin
As flame melts caunle-wax tae ile.
The sgurrs an bens will loup wi fire
An aw the oceans bile.

Cauld-hertit hills that winna nou
Gie furth tae men their mineral store
Will jaw oot ceaseless rivers, thick
An reamin fou wi meltit ore.

Aw ye that lustit efter gowd
An gaithert it wi greed an bluid
Mey slocken tae the ful yer thirst –
In wi ye then, an slorp the flude!

An ye that lippent tae the warld,
Will ye no greit tae see't owerfawn,
As it gangs warslin doun wi daith
As a strang man smoors in soukin saun?

Its veins that yince ran cauld an caller,
Daffin an vauntie throu the glens,
Spew up in spleiterin cloods o reik
Tae bile an brust amang the bens.

Aw throu itsel the haill warld grues;
The stanes o its mountains shither an pairt;
Awfu tae hear its doolsome murn
An the rivin o its hert.

The hingit curtain o the lift
That haps the yirth in its blue sheet
Skrunkles like bark on reid-het coals,
Skrinkin and scrockenin wi the heat.

Aw the heivens will be smeikit
Bible-black an blin wi reik;
An spittin throu the mirk an clood
Twinin raips o fire will streak.

Aroun the warld the gowlie rair
O birlin blowsterous thunner gaes;
An reivin flames burn aff the lift
Like heather fired on uplan braes.

Frae their fower airts the winds thegither
Caw the storm on tae swall an quake,
An wi the strenth o angels bring
The warld entire tae utter wraik.

Sae the sax days' darg o God is skailt,
An brocht by fire tae nocht again.
But Lord, sae great thy gear ye'd loss
A thoosan warlds an hardly ken!

Translated from the Gaelic by James Robertson

W N Herbert

The Angel of Portpatrick

Its head is the shape of the harbour,
the face is pitted with shingle, bearded
by weed. Detergent flecks its lips.
Its wings have flaked to gulls
and flock the cliff-tops, beating
to the tides of carrion and scrag.

The angel keeps on battering its head
on the stubborn wall of our awareness,
as though it desired to be foam
of thought, as though it did desire.
The harbour's shape is found each night
in our sleep, carried like a charm.

The angel is our desire to return
to the embrace of the harbour.
Half-awake in the hour before birds,
unconvinced that ghosts will never come,
we grow indefinite: that our choice
of partner, our morality, was well
secured. It feels like it's slipping,
even now, to new consequences,
below the random surfaces of sleep.

The angel moves through our heads
as lust does, stronger than the seasons,
as we try to wrap ourselves in daylight
still to come strongly through
the condensation on the glass.

We can't yet distinguish the notes
of nearby cattle from the memory
of our father's snores, that used
to toll out hours of darkness.
We dream the iron ladders groan
their two tones in the swell,
we wake and realise they will
be groaning: what would the phrase be,
built on these shifting sets of notes?

Images pass up the ladders
familiar as the orange figure of
the lifeboat captain every dusk.
They strew the flotsam of the angel

on the floors of bedrooms: that
towelling belt that seems to be
a caterpillar, big as your forearm;
those clods of peat that dissolve
back into boots and stockings.

Here the debris is caught,
as the shape of an eye is caught,
among the shapes in the branches
growing clearer through the window.
This is how big the angel's eye
has become, like that of a squid.

Dreams are thrown from the cliffs
as the Picts were supposed to be,
as the Irish were; all shrunk to bundles
caught in the angel's wings, in the brains
of gulls, clustered on the bulge of rocks
like florets on cacti. That black
triangle called the Witch's Hat
hacks at these birds, cuts loose
their crying from our own cold memory.

Someone remembers an old woman,
walking up a path with a donkey,
from a now-deserted bay.
Someone remembers visiting
an aunt on the shorefront, the tut-
tutting of the wickety-wa',
that she was wearing make-up,
made, someone said, from the sweat
of women walking in Africa.

You remember a woman squatting
over a mussel shell, excreting
a large pearly egg. You remember
a capped man, running with a book
in his left hand; a figure bending
over in a swimming baths, long ago
demolished, as though to dive.

The angel gathers up the instances
in insubstantial hands. This
gesture is called forgetting.
It is not done by us, after all,
but by the angel trying to desire.
Desire moves you towards them
as the angel moves towards
the harbour, towards and through

all landings and all land, all
harbouring. It drags after it
these images we hoped to pick out,
dry and understand gradually,
through remembering our loves.

Sandyhills Bay

Everyone has to write their name, it seems.
You read their sand-signs, crunch along a belt
that glitters: tiny or fragmented shells
like china from fusspot imperial kilns.
Even the oil stains look good as light's spilt
between the honking lines of evening geese
emerging from a pouring layer of mist
upon the old wall-hanging of the hill.

The limpet shells sit hollow-up in dark
sand with a pool of blackness in their hearts.
The tideline makes their mess together with
the twigs that break like brushstrokes into art:
the grim calligraphy of little gods
called Spillage and Despoliation.

The Birdman of Hawthornden Castle

This terrible desire to launch out, clear
the parapet and see if gravity
for once, for you, submits. Better to flee
indoors and dive in books' queer bathysphere;
to drowse through page's fathoms, breathe ink's air,
and peer through paper into that deep sea
where letters writhe away like eels, as free
as flight to rooks. As though that dodged the fear.

Here, then, the lesson starts; a startled bird
lacks time for theory or lacks its head:
it only flies. And so the birdman flings
all hope of flight away, and builds his wings
from absent things: the printless Pictish word,
his lover's phoned-in breath. These soar, unread.

Details

Kate Scott

The cook will only use fresh herbs. To get life out you have to put life in, that's what she says. See how her hair escapes from its clip, how her books spill from the bookcases, how her possessions constantly escape, scatter, surge.

You probably think she looks happy. She smiles a lot and she moves softly, even when she rushes, which is seldom. People like to watch her as she moves around, stirring, sprinkling, placing. Her steps are light as she checks that the plates and glasses are full. She sets dishes down on the table tenderly. Sometimes she'll touch you in an unexpected place: the elbow, the small of the back, the wrist. It makes you feel that you share a secret with her, some intimacy, some history of tenderness. She'll move away and you'll forget to eat, following her with your eyes, your spoon or fork raised half way to your gawping mouth. You want her to come back, to touch you again. But she is serving someone else now, giving that smile and that brush of the fingers like the final seasoning to the meal. People here always have second and third helpings.

If you enjoy the meal the cook will write down every ingredient, every measurement. She will describe every step she took so that you can reproduce the exact taste in your own home. Though it never quite works out that way. You can't package the flavour of a person or the home they live in, the way it smells and tastes. The best you get is a faint echo of the meal and the evening. A memory in the mouth. Often, the cook will write down new recipes for you to try, things she has discovered in the middle of the night. She thrusts handfuls of crumpled paper at you, covered over with her scrawls. You cannot think about food, you're much too full. "But hunger always returns," the cook smiles. You don't believe her, somewhere at the top of your chest sits her apple and rum pancakes smothered with cream.

Lucy is the cook's friend. She says she was born in the wrong time. "I should be running a brothel in a town with sheriffs and cowboys and those giant dustballs rolling down the high street. I'd like to live in a town where dirt knows its place. Maybe then I wouldn't end up living with it." She cracks a smile and swings her weight to the other hip. "Besides, I only look at home next to a bottle of bourbon."

The cook pours Lucy more coffee, which smells faintly of nuts and chocolate. Lucy is afraid that her wit will grow tired and disappear. You can see that her character wouldn't work without wit. She is thin and wry-looking, amused and cynical. You expect her to smoke. She'd look complete if she had a cigarette dangling from the corner of her mouth. But with the raised consciousness about health and the cook complaining that she wouldn't be able to smell or taste her cooking properly it's really out of the question.

The cook and Lucy are friends because they are fellow phobics of real closeness. Although the cook often touches people it is always in passing, light and distant, absent-minded. She gives the impression of being open, an impression which people only begin to question after they realise that the openness remains static, that it is based on the thin air of assumptions rather than attested facts. Lucy defies closeness with irony and humour. She refuses to take anyone or anything seriously. The cook and Lucy get on well, though the cook knows more about Lucy than Lucy knows about the cook.

Here is some of what Lucy knows. The cook started out as an apprentice and cooked her way up. She's written a few cook books, none under her own name, from which she receives a healthy income, especially at Christmas. She is also an occasional consultant for companies who want to impress big clients with filet mignon and potatoes dauphinoise. She is good at her job. She is good at becoming a pleasantly invisible presence.

Here is some of what Lucy doesn't know. The cook married young, divorced young. Her husband remarried a woman who never went near a kitchen, which proves to the cook that he never understood her. It always made her suspicious that he ate out so often. They exchanged polite Christmas and birthday cards for some years, then fizzled out into the blurry past. The cook had a lover for many years. The cook supposes she loved him. Sometimes she is haunted by the thought that those could have been any arms, any mouth. During the day she only remembers what he liked to eat. At night she remembers how he held his cup, awkwardly, like a small child learning to use grown-up things. She remembers how he'd close his eyes and tip his head back when something tasted good. She remembers the blue flannel shirt he wore until it was in tatters. At night she knows she loved him. She is content and relieved that he is far away and that she doesn't know where he is.

Lucy is allowed to visit the cook between meals, a great privilege. Mostly the cook prefers to keep her visitors to meal times, in groups, where she is safe from too much scrutiny. She prefers the illusion of intimacy to the reality. Although it's hard to tell what the truth is, or what the truths are. It's hard to judge someone who refuses to stand still, who moves either too close or too far away to keep in focus. She goes out of frame, which is how she wants it. Most people are prepared to like her at a distance anyway. They don't want anything interfering with their conception of her as earth mother, feeder, or simply, great hostess. They want to come to dinner, to look at her and get fed. They know too many people too well already. Lucy is around more often because she agrees to be, or simply is, laconic and flippant on a more or less full time basis.

Lucy works in news broadcasting. She spends her days deciding between political coups and personal tragedies. She is surrounded with rapes and knifings, embezzlements and corruption. She floats on it all, unperturbed and cynical. She is not sensitive, but she is sharp, and sees when the cook starts to crack. Working where she does, she knows that all pain must be acknowledged.

The cook stares at the clipping which informs her that her lover, her ex-lover with the tattered blue shirt, was killed two weeks ago. A silly death. He had been driving through a drive-thru fast food place, the kind of place he used to swear to the cook he never went to. He had just taken his order, was about to drive away, when a car full of teenagers, drunk and hungry, slammed into the car head on. They'd come into the drive-thru the wrong way round. Lucy chose the piece to broadcast because she likes the futility of commonplace tragedy, it fits in with her belief that the world is 'that big guy's big joke'. She didn't know that the man with the hamburger and fries, hold the ketchup, was the cook's last lover. She might have thought again. Then again, she might not. The cook saw it in the paper after she saw it in the news. Although by then she was looking.

The cook's flat used to be a quiet place but now the TV is left to blare itself in the living-room while one radio sings rock songs in the bathroom and another plays the blues in the kitchen. The cook herself becomes louder. She talks back to the announcer on the radio when he interrupts a song she likes. She seems to have lost the ability to control the volume, and when she speaks her voice sounds abrasive and brash. Her casseroles burn, sauces are too salty, things go off.

She begins to use dry and canned goods. "There's no point in getting the fresh stuff when nobody can tell the difference anymore." Lucy shrugs and says "Did they ever." Then wishes she hadn't when she sees the cook's shoulders slump.

The cook starts to unnerve her guests. She comes in on discussions late, making passionate proclamations that veer off the point or simply fall short of conviction because she is so obviously frayed around the edges. At other times she is almost completely silent. She has always been quiet but before it was peacefully, reassuringly so. Now they feel she is merely waiting for them to leave so that she can stare at the wall without the distractions of serving of dinner. They eat too quickly. Sometimes they have indigestion when they leave. They decide not to go back for a while. Perhaps she has been overdoing it.

Perhaps she has. The skin under her eyes looks thin and bruised. Ironically enough, she looks like she could do with a good meal. She paces the kitchen while things are cooking, picking at her fingers or holding onto the back of her neck with both hands to fix her stare to the floor. Her clothes droop on her, everything she wears looks limp and saggy. Days seem to drag on and on.

Lucy says "Pull yourself together." The cook looks up, startled. Lucy also looks startled, as if the words didn't come from her own mouth. She recovers her poise quickly. It doesn't fit her to seem uncertain. She puts her hand on her hip and looks sternly at the cook. "I won't know what to do if you cry, it's not in my script." The cook nods. Lucy says "Whatever it is you're carrying won't go away. You're just going to have to learn to carry it with you, like a few extra pounds you put on by eating too much."

The cook stares at the ground. "Nothing stands up to life," Lucy says. Then she says she'll leave the cook alone a while to get herself together. The cook nods again. They are both unnerved and don't look at each other when they say goodbye.

In the middle of the night she tries out new recipes. She is two people at once saying, "Here, try this, it's good," the other "Oh, I don't know. Maybe I'm not hungry." She cooks comfort food from childhood. She makes egg-in-a-big-cup: soft boiled eggs mashed up in a bowl with salt, pepper and crackers. She makes hot chocolate with whipped cream and cinnamon toast, chicken noodle soup, stew and baked potatoes. Slowly, she seduces herself into eating.

She begins to teach herself Spanish. "Soy cocinera. Me canso." "*I am a cook. I'm tired.*" Her accent is good. She is a good mimic. She starts to read *One Hundred Years of Solitude* in the original, looking up every word in her brand new hopeful-looking dictionary. She reads it alongside her translation, which she hasn't read since she was eighteen. Half way down the first page she comes to the gypsy's proclamation, "Las cosas tienen vida propia." "*Things have a life of their own.*"

After some weeks she remembers to water her plants and herbs. She throws away every tin in the kitchen. You can hear her cracked but pleasant voice humming in the bathroom while the taps gush hot water and steam. The radios get turned down, the TV gets turned off. She invites people to dinner, only a few at a time. Lucy winks and slaps the cook's hip lightly when she goes past.

The cook prowls the kitchen in the middle of the night. She is always amazed at how the room that is so warm and familiar during the day and well-lit evening becomes an almost creepy place in the chill of the small hours. The hum of the refrigerator gets louder, conducts the heavy silence of the shapes grown distorted and malevolent at three a.m. She gets a cup of milk to quiet the uneasiness in her stomach, making more noise than necessary, switching on all the lights though she can see perfectly well by the blurred squares of moonlight. After the click of the switch there is a momentary whirr before the room blinks and settles back into the known outlines of its day wear. She drinks her milk from an enamelled tin mug. It tastes colder, better, that way. It's all in the details, she says. All happiness and all sadness, all success and all disaster, it's all in the details.

The cook walks to the window where the panes are fogged up by the rain. She rubs a small circle with her forefinger so that she can peer outside. She can't see anything, it's too dark and the rain's falling too hard, but she stares out anyway. Do you think she looks like a happy woman? Look at the lines around her mouth.

Portraits of Alasdair Gray and Fionn MacColla by John MacWilliam

"I am the one who remembers dreams." by John MacWilliam

Genesis Revisited

Jim C Wilson

And it came to pass that Noah lost his way. For many days and nights he sailed his ark until at last it came to rest.

And as the waters assuaged, God spake unto Noah, saying, You've landed on top of Ben Nevis, you bloody idiot. But never you mind. Send forth a pigeon.

And Noah sent forth a pigeon. And, lo, in the evening the pigeon returned, and in her mouth was a bit of a bridie.

And the very next day, Noah sent forth a golden eagle. And, lo, the very next evening, the eagle returned; and in his mouth was a Rabbie Burns tea towel.

Truly, spake Noah, I have come to that place called Caledonia.

And when the waters were dried up from off the earth, Noah and his sons went forth; and with them went the pheasants and the grouse, every creeping thing that creepeth upon the earth and, of course, the deer and the sheep.

Then Noah gave thanks to God and built a great altar and offered up burnt offerings.

And the Lord smelled a sweet savour and said in his heart, Truly, Noah has invented lamb kebabs.

And God blessed Noah and his sons and said unto them, Be fruitful, and multiply, and replenish (to begin with) the whole of Fort William.

And Noah and his sons did just that.

Then Noah gathered together every fowl and every beast, and opened up a hugely profitable safari park.

And it came to pass that the people came to Caledonia from every corner of the earth, and they beheld the bisons and they beheld the tigers, and said that they were good. And they ate lamb kebabs and his breaded haddock goujons, and said that they were, well, *quite* good.

And Noah's safari parks and restaurants soon spread to cover nearly all the land.

And Noah and his sons invested in forestry and covered all the mountains of Caledonia with non-native pine.

Then they gathered together all their wealth, and sailed in their luxury ark to Malaga, where they lived as tax exiles. And said that it was good.

And the Lord looked down from heaven and said, That is not what I meant. That is not what I meant at all.

Here endeth many harsh lessons.

Amen.

The New Pairlement o Scotland

Nigel Grant

We hae oor ain Pairlement nou, the furst syne 1707. We hae cum a gey lang wey on this gait. We hud a referendum in 1979, but it wis gralloched bi the Cunningham Amendment demandin 40% o votes on the electoral register, includin the double-enterit, the removit, the seik an the deid. It wis close, 32% votin *Ay* an 31% *Naw*. The Ay votes wis Strathclyde, Lothian, Tayside, Fife, Central, Heilands an the Western Isles. Votin *Naw* wis Grampian, Borders, Dumfries an Gallowa, Orkney an Shetland. Scotland wis still wun, but bi a gey close mairgin, an we wis catchit by yon 40% clause. The Gouvern fell in the stushie that cam eftir, an Thatcherism tuk ower. The ootfaas o thon we aw ken gey weill.

It's been a sair fecht syne 1979, demonstratiouns, meetins, broadcasts, screivins, lobbyins an siclike. Maist o us felt we wis cryin in the daurk, but keepit on dreippin like watter on a stane. But in 1997 cam a lowsin. The Tories didnae jist loss, thai wis wypit oot in Scotland an in Wales, an dingit doun in Ingland tae. Nou, A didnae expek the new Jerusalem tae dawn, but the pledge tae gie us oor ain Pairlement back wis a signal at it coud be a new dawin fur oor kintra. A wheen o us wis no ower pleasit whan we wis telt thare wis tae be a Referendum yince mair myndin whit happend the lest keek, but A think that Blair an the ithers wis richt. Eftir aw, the Tories coud git in agane, sumtime maybe, an coud ettil tae tirl the haill thing roon. Mynd whit happend tae the Lunnon Coontie Cooncills (the GLC an the ILEA) unner Thatcher. This wey, wi a Referendum, the will o the fowk o Scotland wad be taen note o, an wad mak it haurd tae turn aroon, gin the Tories gat in agane, tho that micht be lang eneuch.

The 11th o Septaimber 1997 wis a historik day fur Scotland, the annivairsarie o Wallace an Moray's victorie at Stirlin Brig in 1297. Weill, we wun that tae, faur mair than wis thocht liklie. Mind whit happend in 1979! But this time, the haill kintra, aw the regiouns, votit *Ay* tae the Pairlement. Twa votit Naw tae the tax-raisin pouers (Orkney, an Dumfries an Gallowa). Nou the real wark sterts, an we cannae blame the Inglish fur awthin onie mair. It is up tae oorsels. We wull be in chairge o the affairs o Scotland. We hud oor ain laws afore, but nou we kin mak thaim oorsels.

We hae a sistem o proportiounal representatioun asweill, an that wey thair kin be nae wan-pairtie state. The Gouvern is nou Labour in coalitioun wi the Liberal-Democrats, an wi the SNP as the official opposietioun. We coud gae for sel-staunin the neist time, maybe, but that is up tae us, naebody else. The Tories still hae a wheen o seats wi this sistem o proportiounal representatioun, thair yin chaunce tae jouk bein an Inglish shyres pairtie an thair yin chaunce tae hae onie members in Scotland avaa. The decisiouns anent pouers, the sistem o walin members, the clanjamfrie o the rinnin o the Hous, an sae on, hud awreddie been taen bi us, the fowk o Scotland. We ken wha's Furst Mienister, wha maks the Gouvern an wha's members an sae on, but we huvnae heird on

ythin aboot traditiouns or the rinnin o the ilka-day business o the Hous.

Nou, traditiouns cannae be inventit ower nicht, but we hae tae gree on a new wey o daein: whit we caa fowk an in whit wey, an sae on. Fur neir thrie hunner yeir we hae cam eftir in Pairlement the conventiouns o the Hous of Commouns at Westminster, whaur a wheen o the members hae cum frae. A fouth wis gey keen tae gie the Hous a bigger dignitie bi cryin aw members bi thair consteituencies an no bi name, as gin thai huvnae names o thir ain. The Speiker hes tae be draggit 'wi a shaw o reluctance' tae the Chair, an aw members are cryed bi thair consteituencies, nae wyce in thair ain names, but whan thai'r bein cawed bi the Speiker.

It's oor traditioun, a wheen'll say. Naw it's no; the Scottish Pairlement at wis here afore didnae dae this; it wis the traditioun o the Inglish Pairlement afore we wis suckt intae it, an we hae yaised thae conventiouns fur oniethin 'pairlementarie'. Bein Speiker wis a riskie job unner Charles I (that's whit wey they hae yon 'show o reluctance'), an the conventioun o cryin members bi thair constituencies or offices, raxes back tae yon time tae. Gin the Inglish want tae haud on til that, an the UK Pairlement, (fur the Inglish hae a majoritie in yon) that's thair affair. Gin they want tae haud onto thae 'traditiouns' fur a sense o continuitie, that is aw richt fur thaim.

Whit wey dis a Pairlement in the 21st centurie tae cairrie on lik it did whan a king ettilled tae arrest members (an tint a war wi Pairlement, an his heid forbye) in the 17th centurie nae dout dis nae hairm the nou, but disnae add tae its dignities avaa. This is a thing at the Westminster Pairlement coud keek at gin they want tae 'modernise' thirsels. Wan o the scunners wi Westminster is at they dinnae see it as hou they yaised tae dae things in *thair* pairlement, but thai hae this notioun that it's the Mither o Pairlements, an that thair wey is a norm fur aabodie in the warld.

Shair it's auld, but sae is ither Pairlements, lik Iceland (the Althing is maybe aulder); but naebodie said we soud copie the Icelanders or the Danes or the Catalan Generalitat or awthin else. Nou, the Danes an the Catalans are wee kintras, lik us. The Danish Folketing hes ane auld traditioun, the Danes hae five millioun fowk, an the Generalitat de Catalunya cam intae bein whan democracie wis restaurit in Spain, but wis based on aulder institutiouns that rax back tae the Middle Ages. Maybe we soud keek at thae wee kintras an hou thai gouvern thairsels, fur thai're mair sib wi us. A Catalan frein screivit me juist eftir the Referendum, an feenishit wi the wards, 'Visca l'Escocia llibre!' (Lang lieve free Scotland! in Catalan). Whit we're gettin nou is whit the Catalans hud fur monie yeirs eftir a lang time o cultural suppressioun. But nou thair leid is vieve an yaised bi neir awbodie (the skuils, the kirk, the press, the Generalitat), but naebody is obleeged tae speik it. Thai kin speik Catalan or Castilian Spanish gin thai lik. Awbodie wull speik in whitever leid ye yaise. This is no tae suggest that we soud copie the Catalans, but thai hae recoverit thair sense o natiounall sel-confidence an wis ane inspiratioun tae us in the Referendum campaign.

We need tae mak the pynt that we're no tae haein a copie o Westminster, naither a Pairlement creatit brand-new frae naethin. It's a new Pairlement, certes, but a re-continuatioun o whit we hud afore. Times hae chaungit, an things hae chaungit tae. We'll hae tae mak the pynt that oor Pairlement hasnae sprung frae naethin, but is a continuatioun o whit wis thare afore, as Winnie Ewing said on the day it sterted.

But keek at the Amairican Congress or the Irish Dáil. Nane o they chaumers duis onie o this harkin back tae the 17th centurie, but get things dune, athoot lievin in the 17th centurie or the 19th, even in the 20th. Gin Westminster cairries on wi the traditiouns thai think 'unique' an important, that's aw richt, tho maist cannae mind whit it wis fur. We maun dae oor ain gouvernin in oor ain wey, no copie the Congress or the Cortes or onywan else.

Sae, whit dae we caa members o the Hous? MSP (Member o the Scottish Pairlement) is aw richt, gin we dinnae think at thai aw loss thair ain identities. The title o the heid bummer (Furst Minister) is aw richt tae; whit else dis Prime Minister mean but Furst Minister? Ye cannae cry oniebody in Westminster a leear (but monie o thaim ir thae things asweill) but we neid tae jouk a yellochin-match, an monie insults can still be scrieched gin we want tae, but we dinnae want tae hae oor Pairlement a place fur rammies an tulzies. Fowk will juist hae tae wale wurds wi a bit mair tent.

But thai soud caa aw members bi thir names, an thai hae sterted ti dae that. We dinnae neid the title o 'Speiker' aither; the term Chancellour wis yaised afore (thai caa him the nou Presydin Officer), an it seems daft tae hae yon title o 'Speiker' fur wan at disnae speik. The conventiouns wull tak a whilie tae sort oot, but thai soud be guided bi courteous, civileesed an sensible behaviour. Nane o this maks it juist lik a toun cooncil, it wull mak thaim jist lik onie ither democratik bodie in the warld.

Whitna leids soud thai yaise? In Westminster, ony leid but Inglish is 'oot o ordur'. Maist will speik the Inglish, as thai dae in Congress, the Lok Sabha an monie ither chaumers aw ower the warld, but whyles it wull blend intae Scots, whilk maist Scots fowk can unnertsaun, even gin thai dinnae speik it. Sae, Scots an Inglish can be yaised, alang wi Gaelic, but maist fowk cannae unnerstaun or speik yon, sae thai wad hae tae confine it tae symbolik occasiouns, or gie a translatioun, fur the time bein at leist.

But Scots is anither maitter. Maist Scots kin unnerstaun it, an mony kin speik it tae ilka day. Thare wis a time whan the Scots leid wis stannardisit an official, yaised in the coorts (an the Coort), i the skuil, fur literature an leirin aagates. Whit did the hairm wis the successioun o Jamie Saxt tae the Inglish croon in 1603, takkin awa aw royal patronage, an he wis gey keen on the publicatioun o the Scriptures in Inglish, nae Scots, the Authorised Version. Thir wis nae Scots owerset, fur thai coud aw read the Inglish. This made Inglish the leid o the Kirk (gey important at yon time) an it spread tae the skuils an onywhaur else 'official'. Sae we tint the maist oor literature, an yaised Inglish fur aw official purposes. Jamie kep on speiken Scots till the enn o his life, but wis the main agent fur takkin Scots doon frae bein a literarie an official leid tae a series o local dialeks.

Even nou, is thare onie rekognitioun at Scots exists as a leid? It cairries on bein despisit as ane Inglish dialek, an no taucht in the skuils, no yaised i the Kirk, barelie prentit avaa, an Inglish wis the leid fur 'dignifeed' maitters. Scots wis cried 'bad Inglish'. But Scots is nae mair bad Inglish nor Catalan is bad Spanish or Norwayan bad Danish. Inglish cam tae be 'speikin proper', the leid o the heicher an middle clesses, or onie wha ettilled tae jine thaim. An whan the Pairlement wis caaed aff in 1707, whit did the Chancellour say, if no, "Ach weill, it's the enn o ane auld sang".

Weill, the auld sang is bein taen up agane, an we maun gie oor ain leids a poseetioun yince mair. We kin still yaise the Inglish, as maist wull (wi the odd Scots wurd tae saut the discourse), but fur serious argie-bargie anaa.. That wull cum eftir a while, but we neid tae fix whit soud be said in oor Pairlement nou. Maist o it wull be in Inglish, but A wud think an howp that members wull be muved tae yaise the Auld Leid.

Aiblins Winnie Ewing, the auldest member, coud hae said, first in Gaelic, than Scots, than Inglish, giein oor thrie leids thir richt places on yon historik day. 'A fhir-labhart, tha mi a'gluasad a nise gu bheil an Tigh seo, am Parliamaid na h-Alba, riaghailteach le Ghluais na Pharliamaid na Rioghachd Aontaich agus dearbh le an popull na h-Alba, gu bheil an Tigh seo, tionaill mu dheireadh ann àite eile ann am bliadhna 1707, gu bheil tionaill a rithisd. A fhir-an-cathair, tha mi a' gluasad mar seo'. Winnie gied it in Gaelic an Inglish, but no in Scots. In Scots, she micht hae said: "Mester Presydin Officer, A dae nou mouve that this Hous, the Pairlement o Scotland, approvit bi ane Act o Pairlement o the United Kingrik an stellt up bi the wull o the fowk o Scotland, that this Hous, lest conveinit in anither place in the yeir seiventein hunner an seiven, dis nou reconveine . . . An in Inglish: "I now move that this House, the Parliament of Scotland, approved by an Act of Parliament of the United Kingdom and established by the will of the people of Scotland, that this House, last convened in another place in the year seventeen hundred and seven, do now reconvene. Mister Presiding Officer, I so move".

The Scots leid maybe wull no be yaised muckle, an monie wull still feel at it isnae proper fur a Pairlement, no 'dignifeed' eneuch. Mony wull even say thai dinnae unnerstaun it. (Thai wull at ither times gang tae Burns Suppers an hae a richt guid time, but as thai say, whisky an freedom gang thegither). We maun see tae it that oor ain tungs are yaised in oor Pairlement. Winnie wis speikin for the fowk o Scotland an settin oor Pairlement in motioun – naw, mair nor that, settin it in bein. An that's whilk wey aw oor leids maun be yaised an gied status. Oor natioun is cummin vieve yince mair, wi aw its institutions, oor ain wey o daein things, an oor leids, at like sae monie ither things hes been ower lang ignorit.

Sae, oor Pairlement is in bein, we hae oor Pairlement yince mair. Thare wisnae muckle mair business yon day, fur maist o thaim were aw be fou o pryed, an mony went oot tae celebrate, members or no, whether in Embro or itherwhaur. Thair wull be the chaunce, the neid, tae get doon tae serious business the neist day, an even hae stushies frae time tae time, but, on yon day, we celebratit oor kintra cumin tae life agane.

John MacWilliam

Christopher Whyte

Duthaich agus Leannan

I

Gealach shlàn an iarmailt dhubh
na Dùdlachd, is am fuachd a' dèanamh
adhradh roimp', a leus a' snaidheadh
mullach Suidhe Artair, claisean
creagan Shalisbury gan rùsgadh
leatha. An seo, san sguèadhar, an gàrradh
glaist' na ìompaireachd làn maoim
air taobh thall nan rèilean rag'.
Na craobhan toinnte, pianta,
neo-ghluasadach air sgàth an reothaidh.
Càit a bheil thu nis, a leannain
dhiamhaire an àm ri teachd?
A bheil thu air an rathad dhachaigh,
mar a tha mise, nam sheilcheig mhaill
a' tarraing a luirg trasd nan cabhsair
sa cheàrn mharbh seo den bhaile,
mo lorg togairt agus iargain?
Is lèir dhomh ar sligheannan,
mar shnàthainnean leòis a' snìomh tron bhaile
le pàtranan luathghàireachd is ionndrain.
'S dòcha gun do theirinn thu a-raoir
aig an aon *bhus stop* a dh'fhàg mi an ceartuair
no, sa bhùth-leabhraichean, gun tug mi a-nuas
leabhar a bha fhathast blàth bhod làmhan.
Cuin a chuireas mi t' eòlas, thus' a tha
fantainn rium mar a dh'fhanas mi riutsa?
Am bi coinneachadh nar ceumannan a-nochd?

II

A dhùthaich, thog thu mi is rinn thu m' àrach,
leig thu air falbh mi mar phàrant glic
gun eagal ort ro bhrathadh no ro thrèigsinn,
oir b' eòl dhut neart a' bhuinn a tha gar ceangal.

Thill mi thugad, 's dhùin do shaoghal mun cuairt orm
mar chraiceann aithnicht', gràdhaicht', fàilteachail,
t' àile na luathghàireachd nam chuinneanan,
cainnt mo shluaigh na brìodal na mo chluais.

Ach tha aon rud a dhìth orm. Is e sin brìgh
m' aslachaidh iriosail dhutsa a-nochd –
tha rudeigin a' fàilligeadh dor ceangal,
tha dòigh ann air nach cuir mi t' eòlas fhathast.

Ceadaich dhomhsa t' fhìrinneachd a lorg
air colainn ghràdhaicht'. Mhothaich mi a cheana
mar a bhios craobhan, slèibhtean 's ainmhidhean
ag atharrachadh anns gach tìr den domhan.

Thèid an dealbhadh leis na siantannan,
an dathadh leis a' ghrèin is leis a' ghaoith,
gheibh iad stuth bho ghnèitheachas an talaimh
is ùrachadh bho uisgeachan nan sliabh.

Bidh an aon rud a' tachairt do na daoine.
B' adhbhar mòr mo ghràidh e dhaibh 's gach àite
gu robh iad eadar-dhealaichte, an sùilean,
am falt, an com, an gluasad a' sìor-aithris

mu ioma-chaochlaideachd an àraich-san,
a' dearbhadh gur ann bhon ùir a thàinig iad,
gu robh iad air an dèanamh dhith, 's gum biodh iad
a' tilleadh air ais thuice aig a' cheann thall.

Bu mhiann leam t' aithneachadh air corp mo ghràidh,
a ghluasad, a so-leòntachd is a neart,
fhàilteachadh, a bhlàths is fhadachd riums',
fheum air cniadachadh, fhearg is fhuachd,

fheum air còmhdachadh is fheum air rùsgadh,
àiteannan diamhaire, an teas 's am fàileadh,
teannachadh a ghàirdeanan mum chom,
maoithe, taise, deas-bhriathrachd a bhilean.

Cha sgaoileadh sìl a-mhàin a tha sa ghaol –
is beag der n-anam a theicheas a-mach, is sinn
an sàs san obair sin. Tha m' anam fhathast
slàn, 's mi 'g iarraidh a chur mu sgaoil.

Country and Lover

I

Full moon in the black December
sky, the cold worshipping her, her light
sculpting the top of Arthur's Seat, and laying
bare the vertical furrows on Salisbury Crags.
Here in the square, the locked garden beyond
stiff railings is an empire filled with menace,
the trees twisted in pain, motionless
because of the frost. Where are you now,
mysterious lover of the time to come?
Are you going home, like me,

a dragging snail, trailing its spoor across
the pavements in this dead part of the city,
my spoor of excitement and desire?
I can see our paths, like threads of light,
weaving patterns of exultation
and longing through the city.
Maybe yesterday you got off
the bus at a stop I had just left
or, in the bookshop, I took down
a book that was still warm from your hands.
When will I get to know you, you
who wait for me as I am waiting for you?
Will our steps meet tonight?

II

Country, you reared and nourished me then let me go, like a wise parent who's not afraid of being betrayed or abandoned, for you knew how strong the bond linking us was.

And I came back to you, and you closed around me like a familiar, loving, welcoming skin, your air an ecstasy in my nostrils, my people's speech a delight in my ears.

But I'm lacking one thing. That's the purpose of my humble plea to you tonight – something is missing in our bond, there is one way I still haven't got to know you.

Let me learn your reality on a body I love. I already noticed how trees, hills and animals change in each country on earth,

how they're shaped by the storms, coloured by the sun and the wind, nourished by the particular qualities of the soil and freshened with water from the hills.

The same thing happens with people. One reason I loved them so much, in every place, was their being so different, their eyes, their hair, their waist, their movements bearing constant

witness to their different upbringings, proof that they came from the earth, are made from it, and will return to it in the end.

I'd like to get to know you on my lover's body, its movements, its vulnerability and its strength, its welcoming, its warmth, its urgency for me, its need for tenderness, its anger and coldness,

its need to be clothed and be unclothed, its secret places, their warmth and their smell, the tightening of those arms around my body, the softness, warmth and eloquence of those lips.

Love isn't just a scattering of seed. A little of our soul escapes when we engage in that work. My soul is still whole, and I want to squander it.

Tae Think Again?

Graeme Orr

Let's start with a geography quiz. Think of a small, mountainous country, which has recently been disengaging from its more prosperous neighbour. It has spectacular scenery: rolling hills, forests, historic towns, medieval castles on crags. Eight letters, first letter 'S', third letter 'O'. Easy! It must be Scotland! But the answer is Slovakia, the less prosperous, more scenic half of former Czechoslovakia. From a distance, it appears to be another of the myriad fragmentary states to emerge from the rubble of the Berlin Wall. From the viewpoint of a recent visitor, it is an object lesson in failing separatism which Scotland would do well to acknowledge and study.

Analogies between Scotland and Slovakia extend further. Thus the beautiful landscapes are disfigured by ugly, functional postwar town developments and factories. People live frugally, and there is little ostentation of wealth; this is a land where socialism still holds sway, in both good ways and bad. On the positive side, public transport and basic commodities are inexpensive. Beer costs 35p a pint, and a 20 mile train journey can cost less than £1 return. On the other hand, the people appear dispirited; unemployment is high, the Velvet Divorce from the Czech Republic has given the people 'their own' government, but it is a narrow-minded, xenophobic regime led by Vladimir Meciar, whose mismanagement has led to a power vacuum into which have been drawn new Eastern mafias. Meanwhile the 'big brother' Czech neighbour has attracted German investment in Skoda cars and Pilsener lager, and a steady flow of tourists into Prague. Where has Slovakia gone wrong?

We should decide at the outset which attributes of a country are favourable and which are not; and this can lead into dangerous territory. Prosperity and some measure of autonomy are usually considered beneficial; but the former may bring traffic congestion and pollution, while the latter can seldom be achieved without some exclusivity, nationalism and xenophobia among the populace. A central position in European should help trade; Slovakia boasts a plaque marking the 'Centre of Europe', yet still lags behind its neighbours. Good transport routes and an outgoing people also help to advance the standard of living; Slovakia has a remarkable rail system considering the mountainous terrain, but a rather aloof, parochial populace. Yet Switzerland, another landlocked and mountainous country, has prospered in spite of its aloof stance from its neighbours. Ah yes, you may say, but Switzerland stayed out of the war and avoided the devastation suffered by the rest of mainland Europe. In fact, if you accept the official version of events, Slovakia also had a 'good war'; it was not until 1944 that the partisan army with international help flushed out the Nazi invaders. The truth is less glorious; for much of the war, Slovakia was a strategic backwater, where the ex-Tsar of Bulgaria could live in peaceful exile in a large manor-house, surrounded by hunting trophies and family portraits.

Pickings for any invader were scanty; timber is the principal natural resource today, the silver mines having been exhausted many years ago. The full horror of the Nazi "Final Solution" seems to have spared the Slovakian Gypsy population, still a significant presence in many towns where their metal-working talents were once valuable. A slight, dark-skinned, swarthy people, they are now a definite underclass, although I saw no evidence of persecution but compelling evidence of intermarriage.

Perhaps these aspects of present-day Slovakia offer a key to their current economic plight: the people have been vassals of imperial overlords for too long, and have not yet a clear vision of who they are, what group of nations they belong or owe allegiance to, and who their national heroes are. Small countries, like small people, can suffer psychologically from abuse from bigger neighbours. If they do not or cannot compete, they turn sullen, refusing even the help they need: Albania is a marked example, but Portugal under Salazar or Greece under the generals were little better.

Daily life in provincial Slovakia is in some respects frozen in the communist past. Small towns have strategically-placed loudspeakers which suddenly burst into life with a clarion call of popular music, followed by the monotonous drone of (one supposes) the town crier. Whatever the news, nobody pays any attention to this intrusion – a piece of rusted State machinery, like the ageing Skoda cars clinging to an inefficient, irrelevant bygone era. But country dwellers visiting Slovakia cannot fail to be struck by the abundant landscape. In the hedgerows are a myriad of flowers; skylarks soar, singing their hearts out; the farmland is sprinkled with haystacks, and there are cherry-trees drooping with fruit everywhere. We may well see this peaceful place as some kind of Utopia, but even Utopias need a sense of direction and purpose, which is lacking at present. The more ambitious Slovaks must regret the increasing economic distance of the Czech Republic, now on the threshold of the European Union.

A possible solution would be to create a loose federation of central European, Scandinavian, and former USSR satellite states, a sort of second division European Community. Rather than countries seeking protection under the EU umbrella, and suffering EU paternalism in return, they could use the new confederation to overcome past rivalry and outright enmity and develop at a rate that suited their own citizens rather than some capitalist ringmaster. 'Progress' known in western Europe is a double-edged sword: what progress is it for every family to have two cars, only to languish in gridlocked frustration? What use are computers with massive memories if it takes an ENIGMA code-breaker to find a simple file? Slovakia and its neighbours remind us of a simpler, less frenetic lifestyle.

One significant alternative centre of influence is the Church. Slovakia is not a monolithic state; there are many fine historic church buildings, and both Catholic and Protestant worshippers. The State tolerates the Church which is not equated with nationalism and against Socialism, as has been the case in Poland, and young Slovak and Hungarian men are joining the priesthood, which is more outward-looking and progressive.

Could an independent Scotland become a neglected backwater of Europe? In some respects, we are in a 'no-win' situation in our junior partnership or 'union' with England. If we choose to remain united, we will remain remote from London; if we cast loose, like Slovakia, England may extract revenge by withdrawing investment. They are a larger nation, with better transport links to major trade centres; we are widely perceived in continental Europe as an English province, if a quaint, rugged and charming one. Remember how backward the Irish Republic was in the early years of its breakaway from the United Kingdom, and its continued economic ties to it; indeed, present Irish prosperity is thanks to American and EU investment. Ireland has also shown great skill and charm in promoting its literary and musical culture, and is outgoing internationally in contrast to the more insular English. An Irish diaspora with a clear sense of nationality and roots has helped promote the mother country. Scotland is following her example; we are less likely to lapse into obscurity and neglect like the Slovaks. Perhaps we should seek guidance from Dr Josef Venglos, former manager of Celtic FC, whose contract as Czechoslovak soccer coach ended with the Velvet Divorce. Perhaps a Tartan Separation is a more pragmatic, if less dramatic option; we shall always be able to do business with European neighbours through our own Parliament and trade missions, with no fear of English interference. We have always been a canny nation, with more interdependence with England than we may care to admit. It's up to us "tae think again".

John MacWilliam

Learning to Read

Carolyn Mack

I am five when Miss Simm tells me I have a problem with books.

What she actually says is, "You are a wicked, stupid child who'll never learn to read! Why won't this wicked child ever learn to read?"

"Because she's stupid, Miss." Twenty nine voices answer in weary reply.

She holds the torn book in front of my face. "Anyone who tears a book is an imbecile, and where do 'imbeciles' sit?"

"In the bad corner, Miss."

"Correct children." With that she pushes me into the far corner of the room and throws the book down on the desk.

Behind the bookshelf, I sit in my little cell and stare down at the book. I'm not stupid, I can't be. I know what the words on the cover say, *Janet and John Go To The Seaside.*

See, Miss Simm is wrong, even if she is a teacher and knows everything. I know a lot of words and I know where Janet and John are going. And I know what will happen when they get there.

I like the picture on the front of the book, it's got Janet and John and Mummy and Daddy sitting laughing on the beach. It's inside too, except now it's two pictures instead of one because I tore it. If I open the book, Janet and John are on one page and Mummy and Daddy on another.

I look at Janet in her blue and red swimming costume and her yellow hair, her smiley face and I feel pain in my chest. I'm not stupid. I know I love and hate her. I just don't know why.

The picture of Janet begins to get fuzzy and from behind the bookshelf Miss Simm's voice seems to fade until it sounds like an echo,

"Daddy says, Look at the boat. Mummy says I don't see one."

I'm floating away, away to somewhere nice, maybe to the seaside.

Bang! Bang! Bang! Something inside my chest explodes, my head snaps off my neck and back on again. Miss Simm is banging the lid of the desk.

I look up at her, she looks like Sandie Shaw, except not when her face is red and her eyes are bulging, like now. "You defiant child! How dare you sleep in my class!"

My defiance is a lump in my throat which won't let me swallow. My defiance makes me shiver as if I'm cold. My defiance makes me feel sick and sweaty. My defiance is a warm wet trickle down my legs.

My mother is a grown up like Miss Simm, but my mother is not a teacher like Miss Simm, so she sits fidgeting in the chair, nodding her head, trying to look as if she gives a fuck. That's a word I know.

Daddy says "Look as if you give one'" and Mummy says "I don't give one", or, sometimes, "I couldn't give a flying one".

She looks defiant, like me, but I know it's not Miss Simm making her feel like this, it's because she needs her medicine. She's scared to take it when she's coming to the school, in case they take me and my brother away.

Daddy says they'll take Janet and John away someplace bad if they find out Mummy drinks medicine.

Miss Simm is holding the book up. "I think she may have a problem with words. I asked her to read the next page and this is what she does."

Except she didn't ask me to read the next page. She told me to turn the page and I couldn't. I looked at the nice picture of Janet and John and Mummy and Daddy picnicking on the beach, eating sandwiches, drinking juice in plastic cups, laughing at the lovely sandcastle they had built, and I wanted to keep them there. I couldn't turn it over.

I know what happens on the next page.

I know Mummy has some of her medicine in her plastic cup. And I know Daddy will find something wrong with his sandwich and start shouting, and this will make her scream and hit him. Janet's face will be wet with tears and the lump in her throat makes it hard for her to swallow her sandwich. I know the lovely sandcastle and picnic will be trampled into the sand and John will run away along the beach, just run and run, so that it takes us an hour to find him. And Daddy shouts at him and slaps him.

And I know the shouting will go on in the car all the way home, and even when Janet and John are in bed, even though they have to get up early for school the next day, the shouting will go on. And I know Janet will still be crying when the birds start singing in the morning.

I know all this and that's why I can't turn the page. I want them to stay on the beach, laughing and eating sandwiches. And just to make sure, I pull them apart, so I can put Mummy and Daddy away in my desk and leave Janet and John alone on the beach for always.

William Oxley

Calais: The Foreign French Side

I stand upon this shore, this
half-grey, half-sunny day
and know I can never be
slave to the snake of correctness.
Think how the times wrap
around us, their long vertebrae
of do-nots that make a snake.
So I look at grinding sea on this
foreign French side and say:
Freedom is in detail, variety,
countless as the dull grassblades
or the glittering and gritty sand.
And he is a poet who walks
under every sky of the turning world,
admiring and noting and naming
the ordinary which dusts the exceptional –
for every place is exceptional
in feeling, like dull green Calais
today; and everything is incorrect,
at beautiful odds with society.
I watch the politicians and proprietors
wither in the face of nature –
their empty propositions like old
sticks blown in corners, *kaput*.
And the sea is not crying but laughing
as I walk its spume-laden edge
filling myself this Nineties' empty space
with all the happiness of English words.

The Administered

A city lurches into
consciousness,
light scrapes over breezeblock
and house top

as another day
worms its way
into the journalism and
gossip of our history.

I think of the sweepings

of love, the hopes
and dreams, and violences

that will bruise
the flesh of coming day,
and of God's silent
ansaphone

so like that of
an administrator.

On a Scientific Project to Eliminate Unneighbourly Noise
(a radio report)

No one knows the sound of silence
only what it may be:
noise's opposite, a great absence

like a huge ballroom after
the dancers have gone,
or maybe music of the hereafter?

But whatever silence is – not-noise
or something – it is the peace
of it that noise destroys.

So noise we understand.
It is our own aural smell
that we alone can stand,

resenting others' like unmelodic song
or personal odour. But is that
right or is it wrong?

Now, though, the scientists say
noise that others make
is a farting that's had its day

for aural hygiene's on its way,
courtesy of some National Stealth Service's
quiet technology.

Soon we'll know that silence is
a state that's double-glazed
with endless loneliness

or a place of undisturbed joys.
So that we may give thanks for peace
or cry: 'For God's sake give us back our noise!'

The Revolutionaries
(Mayakovsky, Mandelshtam, etc.)

How they walked away into the
white, snow falling around like
crystals of history,

they the suffering ones. Drudges
of a revolution that came to nothing,
save words of wonder.

Words that thunder down
the black steppes of time
to our day of plastic sunlight

and super-markets grub-full
of a future they would have known
was not quite right.

Kenneth C Steven

The Day the Earth was Flat

I go there still, in my mind
Down half a dozen autumns to the place
We picked potatoes. Through a lens of rain
The fields slide flat, boots suck
Up to the shins in mud. The gypsies watch,
Skinned the colour of ripe horse chestnuts,
Eyes like unbroken horses', their language
Hot as whisky; they'd rather spit at us than talk.
The tractor rambles on across the field
Its bad lungs smoking, then suddenly
Around our feet are shells, soft lumps that drum
Into the buckets. All our backs are hunched
Along the line of hours that drizzle on
Till farm lights start to home the dusk
Across the valley. We walk back crippled
Slumped sacks too tired for talk. Only Jo
Sparks up the firefly of a cigarette
And lets us suck its dizzy sweetness;
Dave brings a golden bottle from his bag –
We drink pure pain and nodding, call it bliss.
I see us still back there, all walking onwards into men
Our world no wider than that one potato field
Our earth as flat, our fears no bigger.

The Deer

Come December they click at nightfall,
When the hills are ghostly with snow,
Flint-hoofed into a town iced by moonlight.

They are whittled from wood;
Sinews of strength sewn together,
Their hearing honed to catch the slightest falls in the forest,
Or know the click of a gun.

Their mouths soften the grass of gardens
Before dogs nose them, bound out barking, big-voiced,
Send them no louder than a scattering of leaves
Back into the huge night.

The Gamekeeper's Bane

Fifty years these eyes have scanned the hills
For any tell-tale rustle of bracken.
Fifty years he's waited, hardly breathing, each spring dawn,
For a footfall, a bark, a redcoat that might have scented
Some frail, legless scrap of lamb.
He's gunned foxes, smashed them, trapped them,
Hounded them – they tremble his hands yet
With an ancient hatred that glows like coals
In his life's blood. They'll steal past his grave one day,
Descendants of the ones he killed, outlaws yet,
Coming back and back from the dead.

John MacWilliam

Clootie Dumpling

Paul Foy

Old Hornie. I mean, for God's sake! What a state he was in.

"Hell-fire and buggery!"

"Is that an order, Boss?"

He had awoken with one blister of a headache. His horns – looking a touch green – throbbed, sending jolts of pain throughout his diabolical body at every turn on his pillow. His tail now had become tangled and knotted in his bedclothes. It took a while before he trusted himself to balance on his cloven hooves.

Oh no, the fires of Hell weren't hot enough for him today; nevertheless, he had the temperature of the sulphur lakes turned down to a tolerable level. The screams of the damned – however much he wanted them to suffer – were putting his teeth on edge.

Ice packs, of course, were out of the question.

"Do we have to have the heating turned down, Boss?" asked Beelzebub, snuffling into a handkerchief. These damnation colds can be nasty.

The Evil One gave his lieutenant a look that could have put an entire Wee Free Sunday school outing of picnickers off their cheesy bites. "You're supposed to have, and I quote from Milton, 'Atlantean shoulders, fit to bear the weight of mightiest monarchies'. So stop being such a big girl's blouse."

"Shouldn't take it out on us, Boss," huffed Beelzebub, pausing to honk loudly into his handkerchief. "You invented the stuff, and it was you that gave the Scots such an appetite for it. There's only yourself to blame if they can drink you under the table."

"THEY DID NOT . . . owww. They did not," Old Nick continued quietly – his satanic wrath put on the back burner for a moment – "drink me under the table. In fact, I was still giving a rather good account of myself at the end of the night. If I say so myself."

"Cause for celebration, was it?"

"Certainly not. I blame McAllister. You think you can trust someone when it comes to penalty kicks."

Looking human – perhaps a little too human for the occasion – Hornie had set off to make mischief.

The bar wasn't chosen with any great precision, but was fine. Just fine: a tickle of east-coast Welshian; a smidgen of western Kelmanian; on this occasion, dollops of Lauder. Even Old Clootie couldn't restrain a shudder at the stench of Central Beltian breath.

Having beguiled his way through the throng to the bar and settled himself there, beer and whiskey on hand, good view of the TV, he decided to socialise and savour the atmosphere.

"Aye, great pub this. What did you say yerr name wis?"

"I didn't, but it's Tam. Tam Cloots."

"Great pub, Tam. Genuine oak bar." The affectionate pat of the hand, reserved for such moments, splashed in spilled beer. "Best puggie machine anaw."

"Terrific. I don't believe I know your name."

"That'll be Billy. Billy Chapman. If you wur related tae me ye could be known as Tam the Chapman."

Tam winced, shuddering at more than the result of a double shot of Glenmorangie belted back in one. Calmed, though stung by the barb of the reminder of the Bard he asked who influenced what: the writer the culture or the culture the writer?

"Who gies a toss aboot writers Tam man? Wur in the final o the World Cup. Bunch o' poofs wi therr typewriters. Ah mean . . ."

Tam smiled wryly to himself. Ah Mr Burns, he imagined himself gloating, Rabbie. It would appear that your countrymen have come to think upon you as, and I quote "a poof".

They weren't as different, this lot, from their English counterparts as they liked to think. Though the disappointment would be on a scale never conceived south of the border. Even the blighted hope of the semi-final didn't create a tenth of the misery that would manifest itself here tonight.

"That wis brilliant so it wis. They get tae the semis. Git Germany again. Go aheed, let them git back intae it and git gubbed yet again in the penalty shoot-oot. Magic! Couldnae be merr perfect."

"Oh yes it could. And will be," chuckled the Evil One under his breath, calling, "Same again please, Barman. And whatever my friends will be having."

"Cheers, pal. Ye can never be enough in the mood."

And the mood was smoky and howling and fine. Tam felt at home. The crowd in the pub roared then hushed then roared again as the match began. Glasses were lifted, cigarettes continued to be lit, people talked over their shoulders to other people without taking their eyes from the Big Screen. Tam had never seen such spectator fanaticism since his own to-do with Michael. Never since then had there been so much at stake. He actually allowed himself a moment of pity for those poor tartan-bedecked mortals, their faces lined with maps of the roads to Hell speckled with good intentions and liver spots.

"Whit wis yours, Big Man?"

"A whiskey please."

"A double?"

"Why not."

"An a extra large whiskey fur the man here, Barman."

Tam sank it and ordered himself another.

"Make it even larger."

"Here Tam. Whit's that sticking oot yer heid?"

Tam felt his forehead. His right-side horn had popped out. Ach bugger it, he thought.

"Sinus problem."

"Get that doon yer throat. That'll clear them oot."

And that was that. Well, he is the father of fibs.

The match proceeded, the players in a faraway land apparently not out of range of hearing. Someone called Jimmy Hill fell into the same category as writers. Tam chuckled He imagined a ditty where the angel Michael joined their company.

He had worked it all out beforehand. Scotland would play well, pass competently, especially in mid-field, hold the opposition, then Brazil would slot one in from nowhere into the top corner of Leighton's net.

Tam stepped gaily, surreptitiously, for auld lang syne. Or was it?

Whatever, he had chosen his position well. Bar etiquette be damned.

"These are on me." Likewise he had selected his drinking companions well. Such trust. Such fervour. "A round for the boys, Barman. And I'll have another double."

"You've goat a thirst oan ye that could droon the fires o' Hell. GET INTAE THEM!"

One goal down, but hope springs eternal. Well, not where Tam comes from. The Scotland team. *The embattled seraphim*. Tam's breast swelled, regret and pride, he almost cheered when the equaliser came.

He had naught but frustration planned for extra time. The tiring Scots would struggle on, while in bars, council houses with off-colour paint-work, faceless New Towns, Highland bothies, but an' bens, leafy suburbs under watchful Tory eyes (though not as watchful as Tam's), granite and sandstone tenements, Barratt red bricks, in cardboard and blankets, blood pressures rose and heart valves juddered. Tam ordered himself, another double, a pint for a chaser and another double as a chaser for that.

"Eh, Tam man, is yer fit aw right?"

"Just a touch of gout. Don't worry yourself."

Tam looked down at his now visible hoof. Nobody would catch on; they were all geared up for the penalty shoot-out.

Brazil shot first and scored, only to have it equalled by the Scots. As were the next three. But as the Brazilian player struck their fifth: glory be to . . .

"Me."

. . . he missed

Who else to take Scotland's fifth but the man who had something to prove: McAllister. Oh, there would be many fresh souls to choose from tonight after he missed . . . again. And the great thing about the Scots, mused Tam, they would always be back for more.

> *Nor did they not perceive the evil plight*
> *In which they were, or the fierce pains not feel*
> *Yet to their General's voice they soon obeyed*
> *Innumerable.*

The Miltonian memory of his loyal minions brought a tear to his eye. He could almost forgive the Scottish race Burns' insolent address.

Through salt water and the bottom of a whiskey glass he watched McAllister run up. As he himself had run at Michael; the angel on his knees, legs apart. One swift kick between them and the balance of power could have changed forever. But the pressure of such a responsibility. Who could blame him? Even the most cynical fallen angel could forgive him the stumble. Who could keep calm while taking a spot kick of such import? But McAllister had to miss. Would miss. There could be no question.

Tam watched him run. A snap of the fingers. A blink of the eyelids, that's all it would take to put him off.

Top right-hand corner.

"YA BEAUTTYYYYYY!!"

Tam's memory of what followed is rather hazy, which casts doubt on his claim that he gave a good account of himself in the latter stages of the evening. But then, we already know about his reputation as a liar. Still, we can be sure he celebrated and enjoyed himself with the best of them; as evidence, his condition the following morning.

"No, I don't want milk, I want Irn Bru."

"In your Corn Flakes?"

Old Hornie commanded that he be left alone. His sympathy for the lost souls was at an all-time low; eternity suffering the torments of Hell was surely nothing compared to this.

There came a rap on the kitchen door that caused infinitely more pain to the head than any stab with a pitchfork ever could.

"Hey, Boss!" It was Beelzebub. "That girl you brought home last night has just left."

"What girl? I don't remember any girl."

"That's as maybe. But she was in the shower when you got up."

"Oh. Well . . . Did she say anything?"

"Yeah, she did," answered Beelzebub, restraining a snigger. "She said you've not to worry about it. Apparently it happens to most blokes at some point."

I, myself, couldn't restrain a snigger.

The Big Sister of Marshal Petain

Andrew R C Hamilton

Translated from the French by ma pal Peter frae Patrick who lectures up at the Gothic pile on Gilmorehill, on Latin and Greek, I think.

Madames et Monsieurs.

For beaucoup de lunes, aye fur many months, I am living under le cloud de mon frere, General Henri Phillipe Petain. He wis always, what do you say, a scunner.

From the early days I toiled with him oan le fields de ma patrie. Wurking sur le grun he wis nae good, fur he wis no a peasant true blue. He hisnae les fingers vertigrease. He wis a scunner mes amis, very gallas et tres stupide.

It is his grande fortuna that I is his sister, his big sister, who he treats like le durt but is rewarde by ma allegiance tout le temps, aw the time.

At Verdun, or as we was saying in le Scottish suburb de Paris, a Verdoon, he defende si stubborn, si very stubborn.

But, he wis a très difficulte wain. Oor maw wis oot sur le streets sae often it stumbled tae me tae drag him up par le strings de la pantaloon. Henri was a learner so slow that we is naming him l'escargot, the snail. Mais tres importani that he kens the tables. Seex and seex is le doozen and al that, for the waging de la guerre.

It is in oor gairden derrier, roon the back, that me and ma wee sister instructe him for l'école de la guerre, l'academy de war.

When he is wishing tae entree l'armée I goes tae le general de les admissions and Ah say tae him:

"Monsieur, le general, donnez moi, gie me, s'il vous plais, les papiers, you ken the papers, de la test, fur mon frère, ma wee brither, who is so stupide."

"Your frère is stupide, you are saying?"

"Oh, aye, yes, yes, monsieur le general, monsieur le grand general, he is stupide."

"Good, tres good, he is le sort de chap we need to fight le wars for les wars are tres stupide also."

And so, mon frere, ma wee brither, became le general premier de la patrie, of all La France.

When the Germans come in the seconde grande war, mon frere no is stupide any more. He pensive, he thinks, tae hissel: if we no surrender we are deed, but if we permitte les Anglais et l'Écosse tae fight le war, fur they are used tae fightin in le streets de la France, we wull be OK or even très bon.

Ah said tae him "Henri, you is a great big skunk, an awfu bastardy, but you is correct. You will be a hero with les strings on your bows and les flashes in your pan. But, if you is le hero, then, ane day they will come and shuve you under le bus. He no listen tae me, his big sister, and it came tae pass that les peasants spit on the grun on which he has trod.

I am ashamed of ma petit frere and wept beaucoup de tears for him.

Then they came and took me and tried me and menyana, the morro, they will hang me or chop off ma heed oan le guillotine.

So, it is au revoir ma friens, et mes amis, au revoir

THE END

Portraits of Samuel Beckett and Greta Garbo by John MacWilliam

Portrait of George Campbell Hay by John MacWilliam

John MacWilliam

Epilogue: The Last Day

Tom Nairn

The Little White Rose

The rose of all the world is not for me.
I want for my part
Only the little white rose of Scotland
That smells sharp and sweet – and breaks the heart.

Hugh MacDiarmid, Stony Limits and Other Poems

On the last day it rained. I wakened at five, with the Lothian sky drumming windlessly down upon our roof in Livingston. In a midwinter gloom, the lawn was a chain of puddles. The birds that usually wake people up on May mornings were inaudible, sheltering in the evergreens or under garden furniture.

"My God, and this is the day they're voting," groaned M., pulling the quilt back over her head. "Trust this country . . . !" (She comes from a different one.)

"Well, maybe it'll clear up later", I replied helplessly; "It cannae go on like that all day". Foreboding has been the everyday horizon for too long among the Scots, never more so than when cheerily contradicted. Yet if you just say nothing, that too feels like giving in. Somehow you always felt you just couldn't win. Not on your own, anyway.

Downstairs making coffee, I could hear that the front guttering had once more given way under the strain. There was the familiar sound of a Highland torrent sluicing down the door-step. As I was wrestling with the toaster the phone rang, far too early.

"Jean's very poorly" said her relative from Fife, ". . . gone down a lot. I just thought you ought to know". I thanked her, already inwardly rescrambling my plans for the day. The tone was unmistakable. On this day, the first in history that the people of Scotland were to vote for their own Parliament, Miss Jean Robertson of St Monan's was dying about 40 miles away, in a hospital at St Andrews. We had been to see her a week before. She was then ailing noticeably, but still in command of hospital staff and visitors alike, and talking loudly of her plans for going home. Now there would be one more chance to see her, and I had to go on my own.

Death in the Morning

On the ridge road above Ecclesmachan there is normally a commanding vista over the Forth, from The Binns right down to the bridges at Queensferry. But on that day the view from West Lothian was non-existent. Round the sharp bends over the Union Canal, the recently-installed traffic-lights winked feebly through a tenebrous mirk, and beyond them the rush-hour traffic towards Silicon Glen revved impatiently, tailing helplessly back towards Newton and Edinburgh. I stopped in Newton Main Street and dodged across to the shop for the newspapers.

Just after the village there is another famous bridge view-point – also a quiet place to scan headlines and editorials. On May 6th these were largely historic-day material. Britain's Balkan war was for once off the front pages. The tabloids hyper-ventilated for Labour ("A Double Dewars!" etc.) with *The Herald* moving in the other direction. It was giving readers a last dose of the grand impartiality which had recently overtaken it.

But a weird spasm had overcome *The Scotsman,* its personality long split in two between the granitic Unionism of its proprietors and Editor-in-Chief, and the nationalism of so many contributors and columnists. Unable to recommend that readers vote both ways at once, the agèd *torchon de cul* had opted for principled retreat to the womb. It reproduced its founding editorial pronouncement *of 1816,* the year after Waterloo. This turned out to be terribly and self-consciously British, and all for the safely New. Hence Britishness – and possibly the whole of history – is culminating in Blair. Now was the day and hour, and the drumroll of antique Whiggery was meant to arrest separatist misconduct among Edinburghese voters.

Feeling helpless again, I looked up into the mist. It would not have been too surprising to see James Hogg's Reverend Wringhim writhing about out there, and groaning of the day's awful portents. In fact, justified sinners of a sort had been at work since the previous week when we took the same route to St Andrews. Two bays along now stood a burned-out Escort XR3 on its hubs surrounded by broken glass and beer-cans. The bridges remained invisible with the rain hitting harder than ever.

The White Rose's End

Over the bridge into Fife the fog thinned slightly, and traffic speeded up on to the new dual carriage-way to Kirkcaldy. But at Markinch it closed in again like a wall. In the villages of the Howe I crawled past two little schools turned into polling stations, with the regulation poster display (one per party) and policemen in attendance. There were few voters about. It made me think of 12 years previously, when I had broken election law by pinning up '*Vote for a Tory-Free Scotland*' posters on the corner outside Jean Robertson's house. "Eh son, the bobby was richt on yer heels . . . He had them doon again as soon as ye were back in the hoose", she told me with some pleasure. "Ye'll never change things yon way, son!" (she and her sister called most people either "son" or "ma lass").

It was about eleven when I got into St Andrews from the Old Course side. "She's sometimes conscious", the Ward Sister warned me, ". . . but don't expect too much". It was a shock: the silver-white rose had been stripped bare in one week, tumour and kidney-failure leaving only a shred. Nobody else was there, for which I felt grateful. I leaned down close to the parchment face, the eyes flickered open and she moaned faintly. I remembered smooth-pink cheeks and brightly mocking grey eyes. You can never say what you mean at such times, or be sure it's heard; yet nothing matters more.

Jean had indeed served the Lord in one of His most formidable metaphysical statements, the Auld Kirk of St Monans. Its brooding spirit and its rising damp had benefited greatly from her decades of bring-and-buy sales. When I moved to the village she knew quickly that I was disaffected from the faith, as from other ancestral causes like the Scottish Conservative & Unionist Party. There was no escape from her kind irony on such matters. More important by an immeasurable distance was the great, repressed sweetness of her nature. The rauch tongue hid, yet also nourished, an underlying warmth and expansiveness. This music of the soul was linked to imperious impatience. Jean wanted things done each day, and usually got her way: it was like having a small, bullying angel on one's side.

But on my side she remained over years of setback and failure, and in the end of shipwreck. In those days St Monans was still 'Holy City', famed for its proliferation of sects. The Open Brethren bellowed tunelessly next door to her, and the Closed Brethren (who feared all music) held their blunt conversations with God at the other end of our street. I once observed to her how odd it was that the same meek flocks invariably voted in a very different sort of fundamentalist as their Provost: an anarchic Nationalist who boasted of breaking every rule going, and getting away with it. Jean disapproved of him terribly. "That rogue's back again!" she would say, "Thae folk dinnae ken *whit* they want!" There was no way of knowing whether she secretly voted for him too. He too has now died; but only after being re-elected for a last time, on this same day.

Were they awake at prayer and dreaming at the polling station? Or was it the other way round? I leaned still closer to her and tried to talk about the days of light she had helped us to know, just by being there. There were others who had loved her, unable to be there or say anything. I felt them with us too. Something rises out of the deepest well of the past at such times. It feels like an impossibly astringent cry of gratitude, for which platitudes just have to stand in. Jean's family had moved from Glasgow a generation previously, and taken over the general shop near the school. They were 'the Dearies' to the whole village: they used this term for all their customers, and everyone ended up owing them something. However, the joint burden of care for ageing parents and an all-hours shop also prevented Jean and her sister Margaret from marrying. Many had tried to pick the white rose (or so it was said) but the only one she fancied had been carried off by the war. Instead the girls came to form a close sisterly bond. As well as being like catalysts of the local community, they for long sought to steer it along the holy ways of Margaret Thatcher, and away from the Provost's influence. The former's fall in 1990 was a terminal shock; I never heard them say much about John Major or the Party afterwards.

Jean lapsed into deep sleep again. The Sister explained the coma would soon become terminal; they had given up fighting it. From the hospital window there seemed to be white rents in the cloud to the east, with seagulls wheeling in and out of the haar. Around midday I left her with a sense of fatality, to take the slow coastal road back round Fife towards the bridges.

You will go into the heaven
Of unforgotten things . . .
Hello, my love. See?
This thorn has cut my lips.

The Finest Hour

Past Kilrenny, I turned leftwards almost without thinking down what we used to call 'the windmill road' towards Cellardyke, as if clinging instinctively to the edge of the sea. The long, narrow main street of Cellardyke has houses practically on the stony beach, and it was in one of them that we lived briefly in 1940. My father had been promoted to a job in West Fife but the house there was not ready for occupation, so we had to rent another temporarily. It belonged to Provost Carstairs, who also owned the smelly little oilskin factory up on Cellardyke braes. Coming abreast of it, I pulled up for a moment. With an inexplicable shock of memory, it came back: right there in the street-side kitchen of this brown-harled house with three steps in front, we all sat around the walnut-panelled radio-set and listened to Winston Churchill. Fifty-nine years ago. The house had gas-mantle lighting, with the warm yellow glare my mother always preferred to electricity. I thought the place was heaven, it had a back yard with a gate straight out on to the beach. At night the sea roared you to sleep.

In those days the wireless was life itself, everyone listened to the news over and over again for fear of missing something, and never forgot the Prime Minister. He said: "Our British life and the long continuity of our institutions and our empire" were at stake in the battle now upon us; if it all lasted for a thousand years, men would still be saying "*This* was their finest hour". One lifetime later something of that hour remains, he was not wrong; but almost everything else has gone. As I realised when I looked up the speech later in the library, everything except the "union of common citizenship with France" (which he had extolled at the same time.) For both Scots and English this still remains some years off, but will happen. At the time and for long afterwards it was regarded as the great man's identity-whimsy, an impulsive aberration to be overlooked.

Of course, what I could actually recall were the small things: the look of the radio, the warm smell of gas, my mother's tears at abandoning the seaside for somewhere far inland – and above all, the excitement of being so close to a favourite fishing pool among the rocks. The long continuity of our institutions meant extremely little then. And yet, this does not imply it was all really 'over our heads'; on the contrary, I see now *that* was how it got into our blood, without missing a single beat over the the generation which ensued. The minnows which any individual recalls are like pilot fish, beneath them swim far greater ones, at different and unsounded depths. Often these are sustaining and deadly together; and difficult to get rid of.

In his 'First Elegy' Hamish Henderson writes nobly of the German dead after a battle in Cirenaica. What really mattered to them too was not race, Leader and realm indivisible but –

The lost world in the memory of letters,
an evening at the pictures in the friendly dark,
two knowing conspirators smiling and whispering secrets . . .
someone whose photo was in their wallets.

But such great humanity can be mistaken too: for the gods and heroes were not really absent from that friendly dark, or the smell of gas and oil-skins in Cellardyke. No, it was the companionship of little things which helped bear those intangible shades forward, and transmute them into identity. Thanks to such banal alchemy, in time "the vague imperial heritage" would seem as precious as the sea's roar or the recollection of a smile. "No such thing as society"? I suppose the phrase's wretchedness came home so sharply then because I had just seen "death making his incision", into more than an individual soul.

Further along, the narrow streets broaden out into the harbour front of Anstruther, which I remembered as a primeval, ever-shifting landscape of herring-boxes piled up to 20 or 30 feet high. We played war games among them, covered in fish-scales and salt, making fortresses, machine-gun redoubts and hidden caves, constantly chased off by the porters and fisherman trying to get them ready for the next tide.

After 1945 the herring vanished, and took most of that old East Neuk world with them. Today a neat car park takes up most of the front, there is a Fisheries Museum and a wonderful fish restaurant. I felt suddenly grateful for change, and also impatient: the nostalgia-arithmetic of gains-and-losses had become pointless, it was time to move on. Time to get back and vote.

Night for Day

There has to be an end to elegies for the dead. The world of the little white rose and all its accompanying heartbreak is gone for good. But in 1999 a war was still going on. Even during Scotland's moment of returning identity, her most important since the Middle Ages, the new day had come like the angel of dusk, overcast and blood-stained. A Southern war leader could still count on that deeper-swimming inheritance, and by evoking it drive the emerging concerns of Scotland off the air and the front pages. This was a different style of empire, agreed; yet one still imbued in popular instinct with all those Churchillian institutions, with the profile of greatness and an engrained longing for another fine hour upon the world stage. Part of us knows we need to be free from all that. However, there is another part which has clings to it with a narcotic love: "Deprived of our Parliamentary links with London, our traditional association with the British Army, the British Navy and Air Force, we would be a laughing stock, an uppity little hive of blethering broadcasters . . . It simply doesn't bear thinking about" (*Scotland on Sunday*, Neil Drysdale, April 18th).

I left the coast after Leven and struck across inland, on a more direct route to the bridge. It goes by Raith, Puddledub and Auchtertool, where my mother used to be taken on summer holidays from Kirkcaldy. The country there has a briefly wilder, uncultivable aspect, the favoured terrain of Scottish identity since romanticism. It was in scenes like those that the exiled State took to being a traveller, a nobly self-destructive savage, a denizen of some nether world. He can be found (recently) in urban subclass squalor, but was most often placed in a Highland fastness . . . "wild country where he's safe", like Douglas Dunn's Gaberlunzie man ("18th-20th century, Origin obscure", *Scots National Dictionary*) –

> Among bracken, in his hideouts of fern –
> Gaberlunzie, half-life, national waif,
> Earth-pirate of the thistle and the thorn

I found myself driving too fast along the winding up-and-down hill road, in sheer haste to get away from him. We've had more than enough of all that. There should be an allotted space for it in the new Museum of Scotland, preferably ill-lit and difficult to get to. Perhaps it might be juxtaposed to a brashly illuminated section on 'Traditional Associations with the British Army'. Both half-lives could then continue supporting one another in retiral.

Returning over the road bridge in the lightening rain I noticed the Millennium Clock properly for the first time. It was set up on the old rail bridge to signal the days and hours remaining before 2000. On May 6th, there were only 239 to go. Not long enough for a new beginning. Turning right towards Newton and Uphall I saw that the wreck had now been towed away from the lay-by.

A vague imperial heritage may stand still, and occasionally proclaim a new age in order to stick in its chosen place. But ex-dependencies have to be more decisive. They have to learn what they are by self-definition bad at: responsibility. And unlike the interminable Empires they come out of, they do not have an age to do this in. If they fail to free themselves, then some fatality like Blair's war, some bit of traditional wreckage or set of blindly sentimental habits will always be dragging them backwards. Failures of state are already being supplemented by a nostalgia-industry, suppurating with dear old links and customs in common.

It's good not to be obsessed by 'vileinye of hatred' against England. But the way to use such fortune is not by being terribly good in England's sense. It should lead to a more intransigent assertion of rights, through different politics and principles. A civic nationalism needs to be constitutional; but for that very reason it can never be placatory or submissive. Meekness and docility will never avert the perils of ethnicity. Civic and juridical warfare is much more likely to – founded as these are upon a profounder demand for equality of status, and recognition.

The phrase "villainy of hatred" was also used in Henderson's *Elegies for the Dead*, as "the great word of Glencoe's son", Alasdair MacIain. In 1745 the latter urged his men to forswear all such hatred against former enemies, at Newliston House, two miles south of my road home to Livingston. Crossing Ecclesmachan ridge southwards one leaves Tam Dalziel's Binns on the right and looks down to Newliston (near Kirkliston) on the left. M.

passes its lodge gates every day on her way to work (with Marshall's Chunky Chicken factory across the road). It was formerly the home of the Dalrymples of Stair, a great legal dynasty responsible for *The Institutions of the Laws of Scotland*, one of whom had ordered the massacre of 1692. MacIain urged his Glencoe men to look after it rather than loot it, in the name of a more civilized and reconciled Scotland. After Culloden, MacIain paid for his vision with many years in prison, but John Buchan surely gave the right verdict on this (the same as Henderson's): "The last word – and a great word – was with Glencoe", in an expression of native and unimposed generosity.

The Voices of our Kind

At the Polling Station in Livingston the rain had stopped. The numbers had built up, and there were knots of people making sure they knew what to do with the coloured voting papers under the new system. As we came out and walked quietly down the road I felt I had been on it for a very long time. It had mostly been quiet, like this. As Neal Ascherson had written of another threshold, 18 months before, "Quietly, without trumpets, Referendum Day began"; and now here we were, returned from the hill and into the house at last – no longer gaberlunzies, the unclassifiable waifs of a half-forgotten realm.

In a poem called 'Two Girls Singing' Iain Crichton Smith tells of finding himself on a late November bus in Glasgow, behind two girls "who sang for miles and miles together" through sodium lights, uncaring who listened or what they made of it. It was as if the words or tune scarcely mattered, only the human sweetness, the "unpredicted voices of our kind".

I had not heard James Macmillan's 'Fanfare for the Parliament' on that day, but did think that trumpets lay ahead – when much of the present heritage has been demolished, and made over into a building-site. Scotland's way has been quiet for far too long. But no-one will stop walking down that road just because we have a government of sorts. In fact they ought to march, or even run, towards the sound of clangour and the promise of dissidence. Just beyond the sound-horizon lies the folklore which counts most, the unimaginable music of the future. We have not come this far, through so much defeat and disappointment, to curl up inside an uppity hive of blethering British whingers, curmudgeonly husks who can go on surviving in defeat only because the English have not spoken yet.

I wish *they* would get on with it too. Like us, they no longer have all the time in the world. Europe will not wait for either of us.

Taken from *After Britain: The Return of Scotland*, to be published by Granta this autumn.

Reviews

Inventive Tradition

Shorts: The Macallan/Scotland on Sunday Short Story Collection, edited by Robert Alan Jamieson, Polygon, £6.99; *Inside – Outside*, Regi Claire, Scottish Cultural Press, £5.95; *The Bonsai Grower and Other Tales*, Sheena Blackhall, GKB Books, £5.50.

"The short story has a long and distinguished history in Scottish literary culture." So the blurb on the back of *Shorts* tells us, continuing "Since its development early in the nineteenth century it has offered a challenge for writers and a delight for readers." This rather bland statement could probably be applied to most national literatures, and I wonder if the importance ascribed to the Scottish short story in part derives from the relative weakness of the novel in the later 19th and early 20th centuries. After Scott, whose massive presence not only cast into shadow contemporaries such as Galt, Ferrier and Hogg but became a monument which perhaps intimidated or over-awed later would-be novelists, there is no sense of linear development such as occurs in, say, France or England. Scottish fiction leaps – at least, this has been the perceived wisdom for generations – from Scott to Stevenson; there is then a diversion to a gaggle of ministers howking in the kailyard, a brief dark revival by the pens of George Douglas Brown and John MacDougall Hay, and then we get by fits and starts – Munro, Gunn, Linklater – to the 1960s and, in 1981, to *Lanark* after which all is, reputedly, triumph. All this while, short stories have cropped up and been seen, rather than in their own right, to "fill the gaps" between novels. Scott and Stevenson both wrote long short stories that have been accepted as 'classics'; and Stevenson wrote several works, *Dr Jekyll and Mr Hyde, The Beach at Falesá, The Merry Men, The Ebb-Tide* and others – which are best described as novellas but which have also enhanced the reputation of the Scottish short story.

Notice the absence of women in this hurried journey. Their role has now been uncovered and it is no surprise to find that when it comes to the short story they are often more than a match for their male contemporaries. This sweeping statement generally holds good for the 29 stories in *Shorts*. These have been selected from the 2,000 entries submitted for the 1998 Macallan/ *Scotland on Sunday* Short Story Competition which was started in 1991. That first year's winner was Dilys Rose, who has a story in this collection, 'The Dead Woman and the Lover'. An actress plays the part of a corpse in a film reconstruction designed to cast doubt on the outcome of an inquest into a woman's death: was it suicide or murder? The filming takes place in a morgue and afterwards the characters go to a pub to warm up. Full of words emphasising coldness, the narrative is intercut with snatches of dialogue laid out like passages from a film script, the subject of which might be men and women and the things that bring them together and keep them apart. It's a fine story about empathy and manipulation and one of the better contributions from the 'known' authors featured here.

Some of these writers have produced less than brilliant pieces of work, and I suspect that, although the competition itself is judged anonymously, the selection for the book may have been affected by a wish to scatter a few 'names' among the unknowns. Gordon Legge, for example, is an accomplished short story writer, but 'About Perfection' is not one of his best: there is too much slack in the writing, and a very clichéd ending. And Jackie Kay's 'The Oldest Woman in Scotland', two-thirds of which is brilliant humour and warmth and insight, seems to run out of steam in the last page or two.

Other stories could have done with some editing but, perhaps because they were competition entries, have been left as they stand. Bill Duncan's 'Boys, Girls, Games' is a good example: it works quite well until the last line, which is "No thanks. I'll best be goin. It's getting dark". As if the narrator has been standing at the bar, telling some unknown listener his reminiscences of childhood, and this scenario is somehow needed to justify the Scots accent in which the story is delivered. It would have lost nothing, and perhaps gained, by the omission of this line.

Writers unfamiliar to me provided the best treats. Linda Cracknell's 'Life Drawing', which carried off the £6,000 first prize, is competently done, but for me doesn't have the edge of a story like Morag MacInnes's 'The Brown Jug', a magnificent tale of cruelty and colonialism set in the era of the Hudson's Bay fur-trading Company. Apparently she is writing a novel on this subject and on the strength of this story it should be great. And Fiona MacInnes (both MacInneses were born in Stromness) in 'Outsiders' does a great take on the current trend for dirty Scottish realism, very much from a female perspective, that is both witty and touching. Raymond Soltysek's 'The Practicality of Magnolia' is another finely crafted tale, with echoes of Maupassant in its neat depiction of quiet revenge. There is plenty of variety in this volume and if indeed it represents the tip of the creative iceberg in modern Scotland then we are sailing in interesting waters.

Regi Claire is in *Shorts* with her story 'In Memoriam', which is also in her first collection *Inside – Outside*. It's a perceptive and accurate depiction of a woman who finds intense release from the death of her mother, but also realises that, however dramatically she redecorates the house they shared, it won't be easy to escape her negative influence. This is perhaps the best story in a handsomely produced book. The writing is elegant and crafted, but the characters are generally hard to get close to. Some are lonely, but defensive, like Miss Robinson, the diminutive teacher in 'Kalsang's Brother' who "in her heart of hearts longs for someone to sweep her off the painstakingly polished floor-tiles of the domestic science kitchen and carry her away". Others, like the girl hitcher in 'Breaking the Rules', are disengaged and paranoid, damaged by society and quite content to inflict damage on others in turn. In 'The Ladies' Man', Neil is the perpetual mummy's boy, a grown man who has moved with his aged mother to a residential home where his presence is permitted as the in-house hairdresser for the female residents. There are echoes of Norman Bates here, and the story only narrowly avoids pastiche. In all these stories, I wanted to find a character I felt some sympathy for, but I did not. This is not to detract from Regi Claire's precise and intense style, but there is an undercurrent of cruelty in the way her people behave to one another that, although it may be true, is also quite depressing. However, this book shows that she has an assured and unusual voice.

Sheena Blackhall is well-known to readers of *Chapman*, particularly perhaps for her fine fiction in Scots. However good a writer is, no reader is encouraged by dense pages of text, in this case 43 lines on each and very narrow margins. I found this book very wearying on the eye. The amateurishness of the design and the author's own line illustrations do nothing to enhance the writing either. However, Sheena Blackhall is clearly an independently-minded person and I've enjoyed her work in the past. I wish I could recommend this book. The mix of unsubtle satire, couthieness and heavy-handed moralising left me disappointed. Her Scots is as rich as ever and begs to be read aloud, but language alone cannot rescue these stories.

The best one is 'The Hairst Meen', which shows where Blackhall's strengths lie. Keeping sentiment to a minimum, it concerns a young lassie's coming of age on the family farm, and her rape at the hands of the orra loon. It's a brutal tale, but evocative of landscape, hard labour, family tensions and divided loyalties, based in a countryside and among people that Blackhall clearly knows very well, and I wish there were more like it. It follows in the tradition of the likes of Lewis Grassic Gibbon, Robert McLelland and David Toulmin: another strand of that much-vaunted Scottish short story tradition.

James Robertson

Real Lifeless

Dead Souls, Ian Rankin, Orion £9.99; *Matthew and Sheila*, Robin Jenkins, Polygon £8.99; *The No. 1 Ladies' Detective Agency*, Alexander McCall Smith, Polygon £8.99

A copper is dead; fallen off the top of Salisbury Crags. Was he pushed or was it suicide? A paedophile has returned to town, housed by social services in a council flat overlooking a kids' playground. Inspector Rebus outs him to the press to stir up local vigilantes. The son of Rebus's old school sweetheart has disappeared after a night on the town in Edinburgh. A serial killer has been deported from the US. He's back in Edinburgh telling his story to a tabloid hack.

This is Ian Rankin's latest Inspector Rebus novel, and the first I've read. It was an odd experience, like watching a cop show on TV. The Edinburgh locations are so specific that it's easy to visualise most of the scenes, but that's not down to Rankin's descriptive powers. He does little more than list street names and landmarks – the Zoo, the Shore, New Town, Holyrood Park, the Pentlands. There's no attempt to conjure an atmosphere for readers unfamiliar to Edinburgh. Readers have to rely on their knowledge of these locations.

Reading *Dead Souls* is like looking over Rankin's shoulder as he rummages through his research materials, or reading the *Evening News* alongside court reports, at the same time tracing routes through Edinburgh's A-Z. I've heard these stories before – in the news, in TV documentaries, in *The Big Issue*.

The story is compelling enough; there's always something going on, but that aspect grows tiresome. Over 400 pages I would have expected to learn a lot more about the characters – Rebus, his doctor girlfriend, his daughter in a wheelchair, his ex-girlfriend – none of them add up to more than reported speech with no variations. There is quite a variety of characters, but everyone talks the same, with no accent, no dialect, no slang. As a result we never get close to anyone. A neutral narrative voice keeps all the characters at arm's length. Rankin is good on details of

police work. Rebus picks up various leads of evidence and slowly puts it all together. He's no Sherlock Holmes, but methodical and a bit slow on the uptake, like a real policeman.

Dead Souls is more realistic than the gimmicky 'noir' novels put out by Serpent's Tail and the Do-Not Press, but it's a lot less enjoyable. Rankin doesn't tie up all the loose ends, which are true to life, but deeply unsatisfying when the only reason you're following the plotlines is to find out how they all come together. Like it or not, this is the raison d'etre of the crime genre.

I've never been a crime fan and reading Ian Rankin has only confirmed that. There's a lack of ambition in this novel to get beyond the everyday, to dig beneath surfaces. The plot's like a board game and the author moves his characters around it. There's no sense of a world outside the plot. Rankin never conveys the horrors of child abuse or a family's despair at their son's disappearance. These issues are grist to the mill as opposed to serious themes. It's only a reason to move Inspector Rebus around the board.

Genre writers often complain that their work isn't taken as seriously as literary novels, isn't reviewed properly, if at all, and I'd be inclined to agree, only I'm reviewing this book and there's not much to say. It's a good genre novel, but no more than that.

Evil intentions and unexplained deaths abound also in *Matthew and Sheila*, but it's typical of this frustrating novel that nothing is ever made explicit. Matthew, for some vague reason to do with his God-bothering grandfather, believes he's one of God's Chosen, guaranteed a place in heaven regardless of his conduct in life. Jenkins shows one or two examples of Matthew's mild transgressions, but then he seems to forget about it, and the reader can't help doing the same.

Sheila is supposed to be a bit of a psychopath, guilty of murders, but comes across to everyone bar Matthew as a sweet, polite, intelligent, lovely little girl. Unfortunately we never come to understand either side of her double personality. Jenkins never gets down to the business of psychology, although both the eponymous pre-pubescents are obviously damaged. There's no sense of what it's like to be a child. Matthew and Sheila's lives outside the plot and the novel's themes aren't suggested at all. Too much space is wasted on reportage of inconsequential incidents and conversations. The back cover blurb boasts of the setting in the Western Isles, but Jenkins never paints the scenery. Not one of a cast of promising supporting characters – Matthew's artist father, who deserts him for Mexico when the boy's mother dies, and the old disappointed housekeeper who looks after Matthew when his father's away – is ever brought to life.

This unassuming novel does have its good qualities. Sometimes it feels ready to take off, but it never quite happens. The story is well-structured, intelligent and sensitively-handled, but it's like the writer doesn't want to get his hands dirty with the guts of his characters. Is he afraid of losing control of his well-ordered, washed-out world by letting real emotions run riot? This isn't a minimalist technique of suggesting hidden depths; there's not much resonance here.

Jenkins has written 29 previous novels and his craftsmanship comes across, but he might have been better off taking one more draft to invest *Matthew and Sheila* with the emotional and psychic depth it lacks.

Alexander McCall Smith has also written many books, more than 40, but this novel seems the work of an artisan rather than an artist. It's the efficiency of the prose, a style that seems learned, not intuitive, that all these three novels share. It's what seems to be a fear of dwelling on things, of digression or looking too closely, going off the beaten track. There's no eccentricity, no hint of genius.

The No. 1 Ladies Detective Agency is set in Botswana in the present day, but as in *Dead Souls* and *Matthew and Sheila* the author fails to give a pungent sense of place. What does Africa sound, smell or taste like? What it's like to be African? I get the impression McCall Smith might know some answers, but the way he writes this book he may as well have stayed in Scotland. Having said that, this is an enjoyable, modest book that tells a series of simple tales effectively, in a touching and warm-hearted style.

The one-lady detective agency is Precious Ramotswe, who solves cases of missing husbands, wayward daughters, conmen and imposters. She's a charming and resourceful character touring the country in her little white van, finding practical solutions to the problems of ordinary folk. These aren't detective stories, though, being no whodunnit element, but McCall Smith never quite manages to stir up suspense. The only real villain is a witchdoctor who remains frustratingly off-stage when I wanted to see Mma Ramotswe get right down into the evil underworld of black magic. This is forbidden knowledge we want access to, but McCall Smith holds back. He opts to stay safely on the sunlit surface of his world.

Not that this is entirely superficial. McCall Smith hints at the hidden presence of evil and achieves a suggestion of the real feelings and disappointments of life, but never quite explores them. The most powerful chapter is early on, when we see Precious's father as a young man, travelling to South Africa to work in a hell-hole of a mine. *The No. 1 Ladies Detective Agency* is a swift, unpretentious read, but like Rankin and Jenkins leaves me wanting a looser, more passionate book that isn't afraid to open up wounds.

These novels make me realise there's more to writing about real life than bald descriptions of people, places and events. Great novels achieve a synthesis of realism and fantasy, acknowledging that we all create internal models of real life than vary widely. It's hard to come to terms with that variance when writing about detectives out to establish the facts. These books are in no sense badly-written, but they share a failure that comes from trying to ignore the dark, irrational undercurrents of life. These stories won't touch their readers deeply and will be easily forgotten.

John Gunn

Edinburgh Book Festival: Looking Back, Seeing Forward

One word epitomised this year's enterprising, exciting and efficient Book Festival. *Faith*. Director Ms Liddell is probably fed up with journalese hijacking of her forename but it is her beliefs, commitment and conviction that guided audiences to authors in the 10th International Book Festival in Charlotte Square which ran over a mind-enlarging seventeen days in August.

Take the International dimension first. Most afternoons featured a visitor in 'The Bigger Picture' slot. Designated as "a Scottish platform for some of the most distinctive voices in international fiction and poetry" this became an overview of new ideas worldwide. They became focused for audiences due to the informed presence of Ben Twist as Chair for nearly all the sessions. A centre of attention to common intentions held sway. Ever conscious of a devolving Scotland questions of political freedom vied with overlapping discussions on creative liberation.

It started when Norwegian Rune Christiansen explained why he situated his novel *Steve McQueen is Dead* in Glasgow. "It is a way of assimilating the new, a way of distancing myself from hidebound stagnant tradition." An element of the latter almost sank the PEN symposium on 'Scotland and Ireland'. The initial Scottish speaker lost pace and place in time-wasting fashion. Fortunately Alan Spence, using Tolstoy as his leader, brought back harmony. With studied succinctness Eavan Boland simply read one poem from her sequence *Writing in a Time of Violence*. It was the apt and brilliant 'That the Science of Cartography is Limited'. The other Irish contributor, Colum McCann, gave instantaneous reactions to previous speakers with Irish wit given the brevity of serious intent. He summed up the theme of the past feeding the future: "Freedom comes from giving into what you do not know about".

All this led both Irish speakers in the discussion after individual readings the next day. Novelist McCann saw exile as "necessary . . . a way of getting writing done about internal matters by taking on external, distancing, even alien themes". Boland was eloquent on "the necessity of hearing the woman's voice in new Irish writing . . . any national literature without this is a distorted literature", concluding, "Writing is about what we make human or choose to dehumanise".

Next came South African André Brink. He saw literature as "a site for recording survival of upheavals, personal and political". He challenged "complicity with apathy". In a rousing finale he stated "Though history is a way of opening or closing silences. Historical facts in their selective ways do demand the corrective of fictions. They provoke the novelist's imaginative way of lying".

German speaking, Berlin based, novelist Herta Muller was next to address these by now interlocking themes. "When I left the undemocratic Romania of my childhood I brought a language with me. It was German, but a new German being written in a new place". This was its "private value" to her as a creative writer. "The vocabulary of the mind. Journalists do not understand this." Doris Lessing does. Speaking of displacement and individuality she summed up her approach "My home is English literature. That is where I have my being". Other memorable visitors were Earl Lovelace from Trinidad and, wonderfully, Anne Michaels reading new poems on the final day.

Speaking of poems and the final day, a word or two of appreciative praise for the Book Festival and *The Scotsman* on appointing Donny O'Rourke as Resident Bard and commissioning a daily poem. In the final event he read these. They are collectively titled *O'Rourke's Drift*. They are gentle, tender and always thoughtful evocations of both Festival and events outwith.

They also articulated Faith Liddell's other significant success this summer. On the opening day, while welcoming the visitors, she declared she wanted "this year to be a showcase for the very best of Scottish writing". She succeeded admirably. However even she must have been surprised that the two most significant speakers come from an older generation. At the beginning and the end the words of Richard Holloway and Edwin Morgan were to have the most lasting significance on Scottish thinking.

As the debate initiated by James MacMillan on perceived prejudice against Catholicism and Catholics in Scotland filled pages elsewhere it became obvious that the presence of Bishop Richard Holloway in Charlotte Square would take on a new dimension. While not sharing his Christian faith it became impossible to disagree with his humane beliefs. Or fail to see their significance in a new pluralistic Scotland. His moral embrace of embattled minorities, Gay or Semite, was heartening. His interpretation of scripture in the city of Knox as "human constructs . . . not the immutable voice of God" had the rationality of a new self-confident intelligence. Finally there was the modest but effective humour. His self-designation as an "extreme moderate" had even the tabloid hacks, assembled looking for a drugged up apostate, bemused and beaming. How we laughed when he continued "I like oxymorons . . . in fact I like all morons".

One could only wish that his fellow Christian the American didactic Mary Daly had even a glimmer of his wit and wisdom. She did not and in a session dictated by self-promotion was a great disappointment for this commentator who had long admired her *Beyond God the Father: Toward a Philosophy of Women's Liberation* (1986).

However, back to the land where even the short-worded morons live happily. In far from 'moronic' fashion Holloway's evocation of *Godless Morality* (his latest tome) found resonant echo in a discussion on the morality of, and in, crime writing between Ian Rankin and Val McDermid. Earlier the same day the former read and corrected his new manuscript *Set in Darkness* before abandoning Edinburgh and the Oxford Bar for Australia. McDermid later loosed a few plump red herrings from within her work. In tandem they showed an awareness of responsibility to 'creative truth' within their genre.

A mild sidestep before concluding. As in the past I enrolled the daughter of my neighbours to help me range and roam. Emma took a bus with Alistair Moffatt *In Search of Arthur*. Billed as 'mysterious' this became a five hour trip to Kelso. She almost defected. But came back to note that Sean Hughes puts on funny voices when answering 'foreigners" questions and Ken Russel's promotional rambles were "boring".

Back in the Speigeltent I was delighted to follow new Scottish writing under the assured (and vastly more relaxed than last year) chair of Diana Hope. Hope and promise became fulfilment and achievement among the 100 strong Scottish contingent. Also, as in the international sessions, common themes emerged naturally without programming. Scottish poets Janet Paisley, Stewart Conn and Tom Pow spoke of bereavement allowing "an opportunity to escape from silence" (Paisley), creating "a responsibility to preserve memories" (Conn), challenging the approach of "words yet to be spoken; the seedhead, hope" (Pow). I do not need to recommend to *Chapman* readers Pow's collaboration with artist Hugh Bryden in the beautifully produced *Landscapes* (Cacafuego Press £15.00). But I will anyway.

Breaking silence, preserving memory, challenging the future–these were the themes fulfilled. If poets dictated the pace it was the novelists, fiction writers, who gave substance to the new sensibility. These emerged as a diverse, articulate group of individuals linked only by a common nationality. The word-spinning novellas of Candia McWilliam found counterpoint in the tightly argued polemical novels of Allan Massie. Then that Ali Smith provided a sinister cadenza with her beautifully constructed long short stories.

In R L Stevenson's 'Precipitous City' there was a linking of Familiars when Andrew O'Hagan read from his first novel *Our Fathers* which carries reverberations from his marvellous piece of journalism *The Miss-*

ng, concerned, as both are, with displaced people and misplaced emotional fidelities.

Present at many of these events was Edwin Morgan, a constant contributor to the Book Festival since it was inaugurated in 1983 (it was bi-annual until 1997). So it was fitting that he gave the important closing Post Office Lecture which was attended by the great, the good and the Irish Consul General.

He addressed the subject of 'Scotland & The World'. He opened by praising the liberating effect of the internet. At 79 he felt he had found . . . and been discovered . . . by a "new wave of voyagers" who in every sense could prevent Scotland "sinking in a global porridge". He then recalled historical Scots who in their time were "literary mercenaries". He found the 17th century William Lithgow had affinities previously unrecognised with the 19th century R B Cunningham Graham. This was fascinating stuff but as ever with Morgan he also unearthed a real discovery.

Helen Adam (1909-93) was a daughter of the Manse who belonged to the same generation as the more recognisable figures of Sorley MacLean and Norman MacCaig. Yet few had heard of her. Morgan read poems influenced by Scottish border ballads which had struck terror and awe into her Beat compatriots in the 1950s San Francisco. An old voice was heard anew and a reputation restored. Space permits just a brief example from her savage poem *A Tale Best Forgotten:*

In the garden, in the garden, while the river
                                        slowly ran.
Walked the daughter, and her lover, and the
                                        dog-headed man.
The daughter, and her lover, and the dog-
                                        headed man!
It's a tale best forgotten, but before the tale
                                        began
His daughter, by the river that reflected as it
                                        ran,
Fed the bones of her lover to the dog-headed
                                        man.

So in the end it is Holloway and Morgan's "wonder at and with the word" that bring these days together. One can only wait for Faith Liddell's next word-baited wonder.

Hayden Murphy

Theatre Roundup

Remembering theatre-going in 60s Edinburgh, I rarely saw any Scottish written plays apart from pantomimes until I looked old enough to join the Traverse Theatre Club in the Lawnmarket. The last eight months of theatre-going in Edinburgh and Glasgow reflect just how theatre has changed. I have seen over 20 Scottish productions, 16 written or devised by Scots, from the sit down, shut up approach to interacting with the audience; from classical play structure to explorations of looser theatrical forms and even a Scottish musical. Reflecting on this and the frequency of sitting in a fairly full audience, like Oscar Wilde, Scottish theatre can reasonably say, "The accounts of my death are exaggerated".

November found me crammed into the foyer of the refurbishing Tron Theatre, Glasgow, no comfortable seats − standing room only. The stage was a vertical structure of scaffolding poles with three acting levels. We stood, the actors never less than 15 feet away, watching Isobel Wright's first play *Speedrun* directed by Irina Brown. Six friends fall in love, argue, separate and experience the death of one of them and the rejection of another. It was dynamic and rhythmic, announcing a writer with a distinctive style. The audience stood with rapt attention as the young cast took us through their characters' lives, in images, encounters and gymnastic, subtle use of the set. The stories were told economically as the action unfolded, inviting the audience to gather the narratives for themselves.

At the Citizens Theatre Seneca's *Medea*, a play first performed in the 1st century A.D., still gripped and appalled the audience. I was struck by how modern the play felt. Medea, lover of Jason, finds he is to marry another and she is refused permission to take her children into exile with her. Medea exacts a terrible revenge. We twisted on the rack of the decision which Medea makes to kill her children, acted with white hot agony by Kathy Kiera Clarke. This production set the action in a Scottish modern posh wedding. Classic plays remind us that human nature does not seem to be subject to evolution, indeed that timelessness is their strength.

Phaedra's Love by Sarah Kane is also based on work by the Euripedies. Put on by Glasgow company GHOSTOWN, the play gained an additional resonance, being performed the week after Sarah Kane's suicide. In this play Hippolytus endlessly masturbates. Those who come to try and stir him to more participatory encounters with life find themselves sooner or later on their knees, pleasuring him with fellatio. Hippolytus with his cold honesty destroys those around him. Yet in this production, he is not so much heartless as a man who has a broken heart. He is broken by his unremitting drive to be honest, seeing all too clearly the dishonesty which surrounds him. Sarah Kane created a play which has a bitter hard force, difficult to watch, conveying a harsh insight.

Whether a play will be performed even a century down the line is impossible to predict. Indeed, in Scotland, even second productions of new plays are still distressingly rare. Again at the Citz, Robert David MacDonald revived his great play *The Summit Conference*. While Hitler and Mussolini confer, their mistresses meet and explore their own and their lovers' convictions and who was more powerful. The tension between the two dictators' mistresses was deliciously played and well suited to its staging in the Studio theatre. One wall was all mirrored and in the amply stocked cocktail cabinet was the gold Maltese Falcon! The two glamorous, seemingly brittle women with their unthinking amorality were presented as even more chilling than their famous bed fellows.

We benefit and are invigorated by re-experiencing the plays of the past. I'd like to see new productions of plays by Stanley Eveling, C P Taylor and others whose earlier plays are rarely given a third professional staging Making great productions is exceedingly difficult and to achieve it first off is very hard. Subsequent productions of a play enables audiences and directors to find greater depth in a play than a first production usually achieves.

In the spring in Glasgow, *Ruth Ellis*, a one-woman play written and performed by Fiona Ormiston, portrayed the last woman hung for murder in Britain. I found this play too static, especially scenes when she was a night club hostess. Having Ruth Ellis's sister in the audience the night I went made the piece play differently. I saw a portrayal of a character who I could not believe she was capable of charming men from the worlds of business and the underworld, or murdering her lover in passion. Perhaps I was there on the wrong night.

The most recent premier I saw at the Citz was *Monumental* by Anita Sullivan, directed by Ben Harrison for GridIron. We were led from the foyer to the scenery store where trains rumbled and the come-to-life statue of the dead Russian poet Mayakovsky discovers through his young Scottish companion, Mel, that the Soviet Union he was proud to belong to is no more. Then out into the open where the sounds and buildings of Glasgow (including a police helicopter with spotlight!) transported the audience to the urban disintegration of Moscow today. Promenade can be a thrilling form of theatre. GridIron again showed their flair for this theatrical form. Sometimes the audience provided additional characters, the actors drawing them into the action effortlessly, a rare ability. The writing also conveyed passion, hopes, beliefs, love for one's country and the pain of their contradictions. It was also one of few new plays which show a consciousness of the changes and rethinking we in Scotland are experiencing due to devolution.

Back in Edinburgh at the Traverse, their autumn production was a new play, *Heritage* by Nicola McCartney. Set in the early 1900s in Canada, two Irish immigrant families explore their relationship to the new country and the ties which bind them to the old and its cultures. Played on a strong, simple but raked touring set, there were some powerful moments, particularly between the Catholic grandmother of one family and the Protestant daughter, Sarah, of the other and also Sarah and her father. The opening scene in dumb-show revealed the end of the play, the death of the young man. The play was partly about whether he would get his life in order. Knowing his end at the beginning muted the following the twists and turns of his character. Issues of cultural and national identity were raised along with the development of myths from the Old Country. Though insufficiently developed, these added to an interesting play.

The spring plays by the Traverse were a triple bill of short plays under the umbrella title, *Family*. First *Acts* by new playwright Riccardo Galgani, directed by Yvonne McDevitt, a tricky first play which depended on pace and reaction. One night it worked well, the next time the pace was too fast and the storyline of a prodigal son too enigmatically dealt with.

Next was *One Good Beating* by Linda McLean, directed by Philip Howard. This was tight and drove forward with energy. A father and his two children speak through the pain of their mutual past and the boards of the shed where the father is locked up. By the end we had seen the corrosive influence of the twisted love of a father for his daughter and her anguish as she acknowledged how she had become the image of him. The escape of his son was a relief and counterpoise to their plight. Here was a kind of play I rarely see, grounded in a specific reality, yet free to translate to other languages and other times.

The final very short play was *The Visitor*, by Iain Crichton Smith, completed just before he died, based on one of his short stories and directed by Philip Howard. A teacher about to retire from his school and to his bed has a visitor who claims to be a former pupil. It was both quirky and disturbing. I felt that Smith's spirit was in the theatre watching. I delighted in the surreal effect of its staging and the unsettling character of Heine, played by Liam Brennan, embodying his mannerisms and dark magic, the otherness which tests our liberal principles. Una Maclean, Russell Hunter and Jennifer Black are also fascinating and satisfying to watch. Seeing three plays in one night is a programme experiment which should be taken up again.

David Greig and Suspect Culture are ever experimental. Sometimes the experiment works, but *Mainstream*, their new touring play, did not. The play, an encounter between two people, played by four actors, revealing and concealing their hopes and desires, was too nebulous in its content. The set, with a rear stage where action was reflected and a front stage with a step up to it and metallic high stools, hampered the action, causing clumsy movements. I left wondering if Suspect Culture is spending enough time outside theatres at the moment? Devised theatre needs to keep in mind the journey to make the piece accessible to the audience; their experience in the auditorium is essentially different.

First plays are hard to write and in Stellar Quines's *Learning the Paso Doble* by Dilys Rose, I felt she had not yet grasped the differences between the form of a short story and the need that theatre audiences to see transformation on the stage. Perhaps Dilys's problem is the converse of Suspect Culture's? We saw three grown-up sisters, their father and the husband of one of them, in the period after the death of their mother. Though the youngest sister sees the Mother in the fridge, the play lacked theatrical ideas; she was only able to converse with her mother in the final scene. Only the character Peg was well-realised, the others were angry ciphers whose scenes ended too often in the slammed door.

Colour Clinic's *First You are Born* by Danish Line Knutzon was a funny, weird and almost surreal comedy about six neighbours and their search for love. This company who concentrate on translated new plays, has an attractive acting style. I wish them well and a longer run with this superb play.

Finally I must mention *Stiff* by Forbes Masson who took the main role as well. The first Scottish musical I have ever seen. Masson played a mason who makes a pact with a Scottish Devil played with a sexy pleasure by Tom McGovern. A Faustian tale with deliciously sharp lyrics (also by Masson) and outrageous angels, funny and moral, took place on a set which gave force to the skewed reality of the play. This Scottish musical showed that we have actors who can sing wonderfully and audiences who like intelligent, satirical lyrics. More please!

Scottish theatre competes for subsidies and audiences at the end of this century but we are getting an interesting range of local work in a variety of styles. Scottish theatre isn't just alive, it's developing!

Thelma Good

Edinburgh Fringe and International Festivals 1999

For more than 50 years August and early September has been potentially the most cultural and exciting time in Edinburgh. This year there was a wealth of theatrical productions and Scottish ones were well represented.

The Traverse Theatre Company, once regarded as the *enfant terrible* of Scottish theatre, were part of the drama offerings of the official festival with two new plays; David Greig's *The Speculator* and Lluïsa Cunillé's *The Meeting*. They both had their premiers at the Grec Festival, Barcelona, commissioned by the Edinburgh International Festival and the Grec Festival from leading playwrights of each other's nation.

The Speculator directed by Philip Howard, set in Paris in 1720, explored aspirations, the nature of values, artistic and monetary and love through the stories of John Law, the richest and most powerful man at the time, the French playwright Marivaux and the then Lord Islay. The play didn't quite contain all these ideas and had a slightly untidy, but engaging air and many moments were both funny and telling, often involving Lord Islay, endearingly played by Billy Boyd. I feel the parts of the play which didn't use humour to show us the story often lacked depth of understanding. At the end when everyone is ruined it barely seems to matter, as if their wealth was but a dream rather than a destroyed reality which might cause despair. This conclusion underlined that all plays are speculations, and perhaps our lives are, too.

The Meeting directed by Xavier Alberti

was very different, set in the present and forming a succession of seemingly unrelated dialogues. One character, Man, appeared in several scenes, encountering a different character in each. The play opened with a wonderful conversation with a wily old man in a park, and as the play continues the Man becomes more unnerving, nothing moves him. He talks only to strangers and could be anyone, a man you pass everyday and/or the undetected murderer. I thought it had too many scenes and could have ended more effectively when the Man talks to the unseen film projectionist who repeatedly steals a few frames from the films he shows. Whilst some of the scenes were powerful on their own, the whole delivered less than was promised by its parts. Even though the script was too long the Scottish cast made it riveting to watch.

The Meeting was a play where the story lies in what is not said, in the silence, in what happens in the audience's mind. It is the high risk end of making plays, not everyone wants so much to be unsaid. These alienated, lonely characters who have interested many writers this decade, have no life and are therefore difficult to dramatise. We have a need to create stories, and when one is either not there or too obscure we will make up our own. The audience often becomes frustrated or bored when a writer seems determined not to provide one.

Alienation was also a theme in *Bleach* Boilerhouse's co-production with Trouble from New Zealand. Done on at Cafe Graffiti, the vastness and chill of the place and the rain and thunderstorms of the soundtrack added to the atmosphere created by the road laid in the aisle with green turf where white lines should be. There were four lonely characters ignored by a non-speaking chorus of urgently walking people but, in this play of alienation changes did happen, as two of the four journey towards a lighter, freer future. Whether they stayed there was not shown but there was a joy when they walked or flew away from their past lives, a refreshing optimism.

This was a festival where many Scottish actors showed their growing variety and skill in both foreign and Scottish plays. Helena Kaut-Howson directed her first production for Theatre Archipelago with *Werewolves* by the Polish writer, Teresa Lubiewicz adapted by Bill Findlay. This is a large ensemble piece where both a funeral for the main character's mother and a wedding for his niece take place in a remote farmhouse surrounded by deep snow and hidden bodies, alive and dead. With elements of grim, surreal folk tales and macabre humour the cast brought this piece to unnerving life. My only quibble was the costuming of the wolfmen, whose animal-skin capes reduced their menace.

Theatre Alba produced Chekhov's *The Thrie (Three) Sisters* in a Scots translation by David Purves but still set in a Russia distant from Moscow. Charles Nowosielski directed a well-cast ensemble in a Traverse staging which worked to the advantage of the production. We were drawn to concentrate on these creatures who seemed to be living an easy life but underneath were frantically searching for a safety they feared was not there. Despite a Scots which bore little resemblance to any I have heard and didn't seem to vary from Count to servant, both the humour and the pathos of the play were powerfully there. This was one of three Theatre Alba productions, all in separate venues and all with large, able casts, a fine achievement.

The Hunting of the Snark at Bedlam, produced by Edinburgh University Theatre Company (EUTC) gave wonderful theatrical life to this extraordinary, surreal poem by Lewis Carroll. Costumed to echo the famous illustrations by Mervyn Peake the production had musical interludes which added another enjoyable layer to the tale. Performed with zest, economy and great skill by the student cast, it was directed by Lu Kemp who with Robert Evans adapted the poem. It is interesting that EUTC's set-up continues to develop talents with flair.

I saw several plays based on famous Scottish people, the most successful of which was *Ultimate Islands* produced by Skerry Vhor and written by Michael David who also played Robert Louis Stevenson. David brought to life Fanny and RLS's passionate love for one another, showing the tensions such love lives by. The writers in the audience laughed wryly when RLS talked about the writer's life and Scotland's unease about creative people.

The Traverse production for the Fringe was *The Juju Girl* by Aileen Ritchie, directed by John Tiffany. With dance and music the audience was taken to Rhodesia of the 1920s and today's Zimbabwe and recalled the rectitude of a Scottish Presbyterian heritage. The play showed both white and black, western-educated and African-born, wrestling with their ambitions, their faiths and how they would like their lives and their pasts to be. At times, it was a joyful celebration of people relating through their humanity, at others a deeply moving exploration of the pains and dangers of cultural and religious differences. And remember Scots were colonials, too. A wonderful set washed in warm light, with a back-lit tree and a bridge which was lowered to be train, veranda or balcony, was so evocative I could smell the bush.

Another colonial past is that of India. At the Official Festival, Ivo van Hove directed the Dutch Het Zuidelijk Toneel company in Marguerite Duras's *India Song*. Here two people's lives, the Vice Consul of Lahore and the French ambassador's wife, are changed forever by a single glance. The play is unusual in that not a word is uttered, the story is told by voices looking back, discussing the events as the action is played out on stage. Rarely do they seem accurate in what they recall, we are brought face to face with, in Duras's own words, "Memories that distort, that create". Van Hove brought us an intense sense of the longing and exquisite pain of romantic love. Although evoked by intense yellow light, music and the rhythms of speech, the smells of citronella, wafts of animal smells and incense, India is rarely referred to by the European characters, who keep themselves apart. It was an extraordinary, wonderful play, performed as Duras requested.

Three of the International Festival productions were performed in foreign languages, unfortunately such supertitled productions can make plays less popular with Official Edinburgh Festival audiences. This was particularly true of *Sleepwalkers*, a dramatisation of two of Hermann Broch's three volume novel of the same name which was performed in Polish by Stary Theatre, Krakow. In three plays totalling over 11 hours the culminative effect was amazing. With over 30 actors and hypnotic scenes sometimes only partially lit and music and rhythmic noise, the director/designer Krystain Lupa underscored the sense of disaster growing in the future. Much was made of a voice-over which delivered some of Bloch's novel as description and internal monologue. This device added to the meditative quality to the production.

The development of the plays and their many sub-plots was skilfully paced with intelligent use of various styles. The action unfolded gradually but in scenes in public places, notably a male brothel and a feast, the increased pace and chaos of the characters reflected a country close to disintegration and despair both before and during World War I. These were important plays to see in the last year of this century. The Festival should be congratulated on bringing them but not on their unsuccessful marketing. The theatre was three quarters empty.

The Festival also brought us *Lower Depths* by Maxim Gorky in Dutch, directed and distilled from 16 characters down to 10 by Alize Zandwijk and RO theatre, Rotterdam. She brought the play into modern day, the action taking place in a night shelter. She also brought in action which in the original text was only reported. Zandwijk works extensively on her productions. Even when a scene works she asks the actors to find other ways of doing it. This demanding process carved out a play where the characters were distressingly real and engaging in their contradictions and rawness. The pilgrim Lukas who stays briefly in the shelter brings a kindness to other occupants who respond at first with hope and then with even less belief in themselves than before. The alcoholic actor who has forgotten even his most famous poem reacts first by packing to go away, "I'm on my way to get reborn like Lear", then later loses faith and hangs himself. Half way through, the inmates sluice themselves and the stage with water, sliding with reckless abandonment, throwing furniture and possessions across the stage with such ferocity the audience flinched, fearful for their safety. Not since Peter Brooke's *Marat/Sade* in the sixties have I seen such an unnerved audience. The play finished with two inmates lighting the many candles Lukas left behind, echoing an earlier line of his, "The fool who lights the darkness". *Lower Depths* and *Sleepwalkers* are two great productions which showed hope and courage in the face of the abyss. They left me profoundly affected, yet celebrating the spirit of humanity.

We are extremely fortunate to have such an annual richness of art forms come to us. I hope that next year will see fuller houses for outstanding productions and as exciting a blend of Scottish and international theatrical talent. One of the special delights of a festival is the ability to see such variety of writing, acting, direction and production styles. Striking, above all in this festival, was the number of extremely fine actors who made good plays even better and were breath-taking in the best, lightening our dark.

Thelma Good

Catalogue

We begin by praising that special breed of Americans obsessed with their roots, even if their passion and energy seem a bit over the top at times. *The Mark of the Scots* (Birch Lane Press, $24.95) was written by one of those Americans with a zeal for his 'homeland'. Although full of interesting facts mostly about Scots abroad and their accomplishments, Duncan A Bruce might have written the same book in several volumes. A rushed read with too many facts in too little space, it seems that Bruce may have been more effective in the 'informative textbook' genre had he spent more time organising and developing his subjects or simply turned his research into a proper encyclopaedia of worldly Scots. It seems to flow along a bit whimsically with Bruce's fancies and flowery prose. He might have tidied up the book by keeping it focused strictly on expat Scots instead of throwing in various titbits about Scottish Scots from time to time as well as people with vague Scottish ancestry whose only claim to Scottish fame is their supposed surname. Needless to say, at times the Scottish factor is strained and backed up with weak research, and there is feeble representation of women and their accomplishments. Oh, did I mention, Elizabeth Taylor is of some sort of Scotch-Irish descent? But to top that she was escorted on the arm of Forbes, the successful, wealthy Scottish-American publisher, at one his extravaganzas in which 1,100 guests consumed nearly a ton of Scottish Salmon. Lucky woman. Consider this an encyclopaedia of sorts and read it with a grain of salt to avoid disappointment.

In refreshing contrast to that scattered chaos is Margaret Bennet's *Oatmeal and the Catechism: Scottish Gaelic Settlers in Quebec* (John Donald, £25). This book is full of interesting folklore, customs and historic details about the Scots in Canada and how their new lives compared then and even now with the Scots back in Scotland. The subject matter ranges from the preparation of wool for dying, to whether hunting was done with bows and arrows in Scotland as in Canada or if the emigrants were introduced to that form of weaponry by the native Indians and/ or the already settled French colonists. Bennet has spent years researching this work, which included many face to face interviews with many original emigrants, where possible, as well as their families. A must read for history buffs and folklorists of all origins.

Continuing in the Scottish vein is Marshall Walker's *Scottish Literature Since 1707* (Addison Wesley Longman, £19.99). 1707 is used as a commencing reference point – a year of 'new beginning' for Scotland. Composed of chapteresque essays the book covers everything in Scottish literature from the inadvertent propellation of negative, Scottish stereotypes within homeland newspapers to magic realism in contemporary Scottish women's writings. Insightful and thorough.

Speaking of thorough, *Eigg: The Story of an Island* (Polygon) by Camille Dressler is loaded with interesting details about the last 6000 or so years of the island and its inhabitants. It is similar in format to the above Bennet's work as the more recent history has been passed on orally by the living relatives of the inhabitants of Eigg. Much of the book is devoted to their struggle to be treated humanely but the story ends happily with the purchase of the island by the islanders in 1997.

Two publications from the Scottish Human Rights Centre: first, *The UN and the Human Rights Responsibilities of a Scottish Parliament,* is an account of an oral submission of a counter report to the UK's report on the International Covenant on Economic, Social and Cultural Rights by Professor Alan Miller to the UN committee (yes, that's what it says). The second, *Human Rights and the Scottish Parliament* is a general outline as well as analysis of the Scotland Bill and the Human Rights Bill once again composed by Miller who is the director of the Scottish Human Rights Centre. These informative pamphlets are excellent reference for anyone concerned with Scotland and her political dilemmas.

Harper Collins is at it again with two pocket sized guides to Edinburgh and Glasgow entitled, in turn, *Edinburgh the Best! The One True Guide* and *Glasgow the Best! The One True Guide* (£5.99). Short and sweet they are pretty much indistinguishable from other mini-guides except perhaps by their colour coded subject organisation.

Published by the Scottish Sculpture Trust and edited by Lisa Bratton, *Brilliant Cacophony* is an interesting clutter of political and literary writings about the history of Edinburgh's architecture around the Royal Mile and how this history has led to the present state of architectural and artistic affairs. Some of the writings are relevant to the architectural and artistic development and are interesting from a historical perspective, while other pieces don't quite fit into the overall scheme of the work and the result is a patchwork of eclectic attempts at artiness. All of this leads up to the finished product of the book's thesis which is shown in an amazing array of black and white photographs by Robin Gillanders of points of interest along the Royal Mile. It is these photographs that make the book worthwhile.

Taking a slightly different turn is Zbigniew Kotowicz's *R D Laing and the Path of Anti-Psychiatry*. This book is part of a series entitled, *Makers of Modern Psychotherapy* by Routledge. A fascinating introduction to the Glaswegian anti-psychiatrist's philosophies and theories. *Learning to Look at Paintings* by Mary Acton (Routledge) is a lovely beginners book for the examination and analysis of the more well-known artists' works from the fifteenth century on up to the twentieth century. A disappointing lack of women artists as they aren't among the 'well known'; sadly it's too late for any excuses.

Fortunate for those of us who do not speak Gaelic *Moch Is Anmoch: Gaelic Poems* by Donald A MacNeill and other Colonsay Bards is translated by Alastair MacNeill Scouller (House of Lochar, £6.99). Although both the English and Gaelic are reproduced here, to the illiterate of Gaelic these poems seem to be overly simple folk tales as their translations into English are literal without poetic verse in mind. Rewarding for those with knowledge of Gaelic and a keen interest in romanticised island life.

More rewarding for those craving poetic prowess is *Departures: The Houseman Society National Poetry Competition 1997-1998* (Houseman Society, £5.00). A fine selection of international tasting poems by 'unknown poets' on farewells of varied sorts. Included in this chapbook are the first prize winners, runners up, and also those worthy of mention but no cash advance, a nice consideration for beginners needing exposure. An interesting side note on the realm of literary contests is that the first prize was split between two men, although the judges considered one a bit better than the other, allotting him 60% of the prize while the second best first prize was rewarded the remaining 40%.

Next we have *Robert Burns: The Lost Poems* by Patrick Scott Hogg (Clydeside Press, £7.95). Hogg guides the reader through many poems previously published anonymously in Burns' time in journals and newspapers with the task of pointing out why they might or might not be the poems of Burns. His clues to find the truth? Comparing the mystery poems' form and content to Burns' known works, of course. The vocabulary and grammar trick proves to be invaluable for Hogg's clever book on Burns.

Moving from to fiction is Hugh McBain's *Man's Book* (Jordan Books £5.95), a futuristic fictional piece set near the end of the second millennium. Refreshing for its genre in that it is entirely tangible in content and form.

For a lovely finale is Violet Jacob's doubled-up *Flemington and Tales from Angus* by Canongate (£7.99). An excellent score for unearthing Jacob but this book could use more handsome packaging, even if the dour-looking fellow gazing out from the cover is the ancestor of Jacob after whom she based her character Flemington. Leading up to the classic Flemington and twisting the title of the double feature are *Tales from Angus*, sometimes known as *Songs from Angus*, a wonderful collection of short stories set in rural Scotland which may lead some to using the convenient wee glossary of Scots located in the rear of the text. For a final comment, anyone interested in Jacob, please note that in The Women's Forum of *Chapman*, issues 74-75, Sarah Bing discusses Jacob and her use of autobiography in *Flemington* and various stories from her collection *Tales from Angus* in her article 'Autobiography in the Work of Violet Jacob'.

Hannah Eckberg

Response

Usually I do not comment on reviews of books, but by its offensive nature I believe Rab Fulton's assessment of *Sing Frae the Hert – The Literary Criticism of Alexander Scott* (Scottish Cultural Press), which I edited, merits a response. I am grateful to *Chapman* for the opportunity to do so.

Robert Garioch used to stress that the reviewer's first duty was as reporter; the detailing of facts providing an accurate summary of what had been read. The review should inform about as the purpose of the book and the reason for its publication. It is only after doing this that the critic can move on to consideration of the work.

Mr Fulton fell at the first hurdle. He fails to inform us that these essays were drawn from the weekly column Alexander Scott wrote for the *Scots Independent* between January 1968 and February 1970, and that this selection of 30 pieces was published to celebrate the 70th anniversary of the paper. Perhaps Fulton read just my introduction, followed by the first item from Scott, as these are the only parts of the text from which he quotes.

When Alexander Scott introduced a bit of humour into his column through a reference to "resident aliens" holding directorial posts in Scottish theatres he was highlighting a serious problem which still prevents much indigenous drama from ever reaching the stage. I give two examples; Robert Silver's play *The Bruce* did not receive a production until forty years after it was written and none of Scott's own plays have been performed since 1965.

For Mr Fulton to equate the promotion of one's own culture with racism is ludicrous. The suggestion that we place Scott's work next to *Mein Kampf* is a slur on the memory of a fine man whose poetry clearly shows a hatred of brutally enforced human suffering. As a young man, Scott, at considerable emotional and physical cost fought the Nazis and was awarded the Military Cross.

Neil MacCallum

Notes on Contributors

Hugh Bryden: born Dumfries 1950. A prolific Printmaker on a small and large scale. He particularly enjoys colaborating with writers.

Dugald Buchanan (1716-68) was born at Strathyre, the son of a miller. He became an intinerant schoolteacher, based at Kinloch Rannoch from 1753 until his death in 1768. His 'spiritual songs' were published in 1767.

Angus Calder's latest book is Wars, an anthology of prose and verse about warfare in 20th century Europe, recently published by Penguin.

Frances Campbell: semi-successful freelance journalist turned helpline advisor. Her first novel *The Past is Another Country* (Citron Press) is due out at the end of October.

Des Dillon is a poet, novelist and screenwriter. Born 1960 in Coatbridge, educated at Strathclyde Uni, he is currently Writer-in-Residence for South-East Glasgow.

Hannah Ekberg has just finished her BA in English at Illinois State University, has volunteered at *Chapman*, worked for the National Museum of Scotland and is now taking time off to see Scotland before deciding what to do next.

Paul Foy is a native Glasgwegian who now lives and works as a teacher in Aberdeen. He has had poetry and prose published in *Mica* and *New Writing Scotland*.

Thelma Good: published writer and theatregoer. She has acted, devised and produced plays and written others. Dyslexic, computers have empowered her writing.

Nigel Grant is Pofessor Emeritus of Education at the University of Glasgow. He has published books and articles on international education and on Scotland, and since retiring has written articles and poetry, mostly in English but others in Gaelic and Scots.

John Gunn lives in Edinburgh and also pursues interests in photography and screenprinting and the Printmakers Workshop.

Andrew Hamilton: professional production engineer. Arts graduate of Glasgow University after retiral. Now immersed in writing humorous comment on life. Enjoying twilight. Envy of literary friends – being published in *Chapman*.

W N Herbert's recent collection *The Laurelude* (Bloodaxe) received a SAC Book Award.

Helen Lamb: stories have appeared in various magazine and anthologies, also Radio 4, RTE, Radio Scotland. Poetry collection, *Strange Fish*, recently published by Duende.

Neil R MacCallum is a poet and critic who edited *Lallans* for 3 years. When his first collection appeared in 1991 George Bruce recognised "A mind and a voice to be heeded."

Caroline Mack lives in Glasgow. She works for a community newspaper in Possilpark. She was shortlisted for the Ian St James Award last year. This is her fourth published story.

Hayden Murphy: born in 1945, Dublin. Poet and arts journalist based in Edinburgh. Editor of the unique literary broadsheet *Broadsheet*.

Tom Nairn's *After Britain: The Return of Scotland* is to be published by Granta Books this autumn.

Graeme Orr divides his time between Glasgow (Garnethill) and Edinburgh (Marchmont). When not designing structures, he likes to read, write, dream, jog and cook, though not simultaneously.

William Oxley has published many books of poetry and prose. In 1994 Salzburg University Press published his *Collected Longer Poems*, and in 1997 Rockingham Press published a volume of short poems, *The Green Crayon Man*.

Tom Pow's most recent collection was *Red Letter Day* (Bloodaxe). *Landscapes* was launched by Cacafuego Press at this year's Edinburgh Book Festival.

James Roberston is a poet, editor and short story writer. His first novel *The Fanatic*, will be published in 2000 by Fourth Estate.

Kate Scott completed a MLitt in Creative Writing at St Andrews University in 1996. Her short fiction and poetry has appeared in publications in the UK and abroad. She is currently working on her first novel.

Kenneth C Steven is a novelist, poet and children's author. Living and working in Dunkeld. His latest title is a handbook for poets on the whole business of getting into print.

Christopher Whyte is publishing his third novel *The Gay Decameron* with Gollancz this spring.